With Borges on an Ordinary Evening in Buenos Aires | *A Memoir*

University of Illinois Press | Urbana and Chicago

With

Borges

on an

Ordinary

Evening

in

Buenos

Aires

 *A Memoir*

Willis Barnstone

Illustration on p. 180 is from *Atlas*, by Jorge Luis Borges with Maria Kodama. © 1984 by Editorial Sudamericana S.A. English translation © 1985 by Anthony Kerrigan. Used by permission of the publisher, Dutton, an imprint of New American Library, a division of Penguin Books USA Inc.

© 1993 by the Board of Trustees of the University of Illinois
Manufactured in the United States of America
C 5 4 3 2 1

This book is printed on acid-free paper.

Library of Congress Cataloging-in-Publication Data

Barnstone, Willis, 1927–
    With Borges on an ordinary evening in Buenos Aires : a memoir / Willis Barnstone.
        p.   cm.
    Includes bibliographical references and index.
    ISBN 0-252-01888-5 (cl)
    1. Borges, Jorge Luis, 1899–1986. I. Title.
PQ7797.B635Z627   1993
868 – dc20   91-45154
                                                            CIP

for Anthony Kerrigan
friend and maker of Jorge Luis Borges
in his English habit

Contents

Acknowledgments

Some parts of this book have appeared in the *Chicago Review* and *Holiday Magazine,* and some of the poems in translation in *The American Poetry Review, Borges at Eighty* (Indiana University Press), *Chicago Review, Boulevard, California Quarterly, Modern European Poetry* (Bantam Books), *New Letters,* and *Twenty-four Conversations with Jorge Luis Borges* (Grove Press).

I wish to express thanks to María Kodama for her friendship in Argentina and in cities of America, and for being there to be centrally remembered; and to Borges for being Borges.

The Voice of the Blindman

This penumbra is slow and gives no pain;
it flows down a mild slope
and looks like eternity.
  "In Praise of Shadow"

Borges had already lost his sight in 1968, when we first met backstage in the Kaufman Auditorium of the Poetry Center in New York. The reading was over, there was a hubbub around us, but as soon as we began to talk we were alone. As he took my hand, I shouted a bit because of the crowd noise, but he said, "*Piano, piano,* I'm not deaf." From childhood Borges had poor eyesight, but in the early '50s he suffered detached retinas, leaving him sightless in his left eye, which looked almost normal. In his deformed right eye he had about six inches of visible yellow blur, enough to read his gold watch.

Now, after a bilingual poetry reading in which each poem had been read in English, then Spanish, followed by the poet's commentary, Borges was standing backstage, alone, without his blindman's cane, looking around eagerly through his unfocused eyes for the next encounter, and smiling. The poet looked lost, a condition he was used to and accepted with interest.

The Spanish historian Juan Marichal had asked me to arrange this reading. I was standing a few feet from Borges (whom I had known only through correspondence) and chatting with a friend, Norman Thomas di Giovanni, one of the readers. Norman turned to Borges and said, "Here is Barnstone. He is the guilty one who started all this noise."

Immediately we fell to it, as if continuing a conversation begun years earlier. We talked about doubles, the two Machados, the many Pessoas, and what happened to the Gnostics in Syria and Alexandria. He was saying, "The Kabbalists, mind you, saw the Bible not as a classic, not an orderly 'frigate' as the word *classis* means in Latin, but as an absolute book with infinite meaning. I suppose Johannes Scotus

Erigena said it best when he compared the Bible's infinite meaning to the iridescent plumage of the peacock."

"If the Bible is peacock feathers, what kind of bird are you?" I asked.

"I am the bird *egg*, in its Buenos Aires nest, unhatched, gladly unseen by anyone with discrimination, and I emphatically hope it will stay that way!"

Talk with Borges was a duel of intimacies, and wondrous.

In the parable "Borges and I," the author describes an increasingly public writer and a sensitive private brooder. The key to the figures is their ultimate commingling. Their confusion and apparent sameness are disheartening yet accepted by the shy one who likes maps, eighteenth-century typography, and the taste of coffee; who would prefer his life to be not one of literary stages and passages in encyclopedias, but a flight to oblivion, a rehearsal of the other soundless eternity. This withdrawn Borges prefers the serenity of Fray Luis de León's Virgilian retreat, would choose a "hidden path and unknown light" rather than the mythic city of the public man who contrives and becomes his books.

But the Borges double I perceived was neither the public nor the private man of the parable. Rather, he was a voice, a double voice: the *written* one heard in all his writings, and the *spoken* one of the blindman heard in rooms, the voice of the friend, of the gentleman caning the streets of Buenos Aires. During the years I knew him I was constantly surprised by the way the poet gave his voice away. After a lecture, in a car, in a restaurant, he spoke unfailingly to each unseen and unknown person with intimacy and with an elevating assumption of confidence, whether the speaker addressing him was a journalist, a doorman, a student, a writer, a clerk. These two voices, like the two figures in "Borges and I," also join and are ultimately one. Perhaps lurking somewhere is a parable that may be even more pertinent to this Borges I knew, a parable called "Pen and Tongue," figuring Borges's written and spoken voices. Ultimately the pen and the tongue also commingle, and the piece would have to end, "I don't know whether the pen or my tongue is speaking these words."

The two related voices derive from a single generating source. His conversation was merely an oral disclosure of the same creative activity that concluded in written texts. And his midlife blindness clarified the union of tongue and pen. When Borges went blind, he had to dictate his writings. Thereafter he spoke the texts he would publish through the same voice that in personal life was Borges the speaking friend.

So, spoofing or grave, laughing or weary, Borges spoke literature. Whether you were chatting with him in Maxim's restaurant in Buenos Aires, up from Maipú Street, where there was good food (and usually a few aging German and Austrian Nazis hanging out at the back tables), or you were with him for hours on a plane, or he confided in you after midnight in the Saint James Café on Córdoba Street, his speech was literature. I mean not that he was talking about literature—one of his preferred "habits"—but that his voice was already print. Rarely did a sentence pass his lips that should not have found itself on some page for the rest of us to savor. He said to me his English was bookish, and it was; yet not because it was stilted or unnatural, or derived from books, but because, like his speech in Spanish, it was unfailingly worthy of print.

Borges's speech authenticated his writing, his writing his speech. To have heard him was to read him. And thereafter, to read him was to hear him. Even on the last day on his deathbed, when he uttered, "This is the happiest day of my life," his words in life and art were kindred.

Because I had the luck to hear Borges's voices for some two decades, when I was asked to write a book of memoirs, I accepted. My first reaction was worthy of Borges's professed cowardice. He was fond of asserting that he was a physical coward, a fact confirmed by his doctor and dentist. All quite untrue. I had earlier written a forty-page memoir, "With Borges in China," to preface a Spanish translation of *Borges at Eighty,* and I gave it to the publisher, hoping it would help keep the English edition alive. My cowardice consisted in offering to edit a book of memoirs by important literary friends of Borges, rather than to put down what I could on my own. Yet that same weekend, without reason or calculation, I began to write, and a madness of memory and pleasure took hold of me. Ever since that first absurdly chaotic backstage meeting, twenty years earlier, I was filled with the presence and words of Jorge Luis Borges, and with memories.

Had I been blessed with Cardinal Matteo Ricci's memory palace or with Borges's astonishing "Funes the Memorious" ink-blotter mind,

I would not have succumbed to initial doubt. But soon I boiled over and for some twenty days forgot regular sleep. Yet it was perhaps appropriate to be between dream and waking while thinking about Borges, who even in the first poems of *Fervor of Buenos Aires,* and increasingly in his last volumes of poetry, became the Chuang-tzu of our time, asking himself, like the ancient Taoist, whether he dreamt he was a butterfly or whether he was the butterfly's dream. Borges tells us of such moments in "The Dream":

> When the midnight clocks prodigally
> Strike in expanding time,
> I drift farther than those oarsmen of Odysseus
> Down to waters of dream inaccessible
> To human memory.
> In this submerged region I salvage images
> I can't understand:
> Herbs of elemental botany,
> Maybe a distinct race of animals,
> Dialogues with the dead,
> Faces that are really masks,
> Words in ancient tongues,
> And sometimes an incomparable horror
> That day drops on us.
> I am everyone or no one. I am the other
> Who I don't know I am, who has looked
> Into that other dream, into my vigil.
> He judges it
> In resignation and smiling.
> Resigned and smiling.

As stone and moon in Spinoza long to be stone and moon, Borges longed to explore the metaphysics of his dream or nightmare, or the secular ecstasy of otherness. He invented personages to be his dream. In *The Cipher,* a volume of poems published in 1981, he created an enigmatic René Descartes who indeed doubted his own existence. Now the real Descartes of *je pense, donc je suis* was playing a circular syllogistic game, leading not only to proof of his existence but eventually to God's, which Borges could never accept unless it was Spinoza's pantheistic all, holding everything together: the stones, the people, their temporal souls, the map of all stars, the God that Portuguese

Jew in Holland constructed out of nothingness, imposing the infinite on his blank manuscript:

Baruch Spinoza

A haze of gold, the Occident lights up
The window. Now, the assiduous manuscript
Is waiting, weighed down with the infinite.
Someone is building God in a dark cup.
A man engenders God. He is a Jew
With saddened eyes and lemon-colored skin;
Time carries him the way a leaf, dropped in
A river, is borne off by waters to
Its end. No matter. The magician moved
Carves out his God with fine geometry;
From his disease, from nothing, he's begun
To construct God, using the word. No one
Is granted such prodigious love as he:
The love that has no hope of being loved.

Borges was curious about eternity, about the names and face of God, and through his many masks he looked for and brought us tantalizingly close to revelation. In the end, however, he left the unsayable word in mystery. So the Chinese emperor's slave poet, who is about to utter the word containing the universe, must be executed, and Borges's ancestor Francisco de Laprida in "The Conjectural Poem" dies as he "discovers the key to all his years." Borges's characters know something, "glimpse the riddle," but will not reveal it to Borges or to us. The notion of the silence of the sound that contains the sum total of the universe is stated in the paradox of the Taoist maxim: one who speaks does not know; one who knows does not speak.

From the investment of wisdom in the silence of sound, we move naturally to another sense, to the investment of vision in the absence of sight. Borges's blindness, his patience in time of blindness, gave him solitude, another sense of time, and blurred the distinction between levels of consciousness. These merging realms of dream and waking are focused in the more serious Descartes whom he created in a poem:

Perhaps I had no yesterday, perhaps I was not born.
Perhaps I dream of having dreamt.

I feel a little cold, a little fearful.
Night is on the Danube.
I will go on dreaming of Descartes . . .

("Descartes," La cifra, 17)

Serious, yes, but precisely at such moments Borges is never reluctant to create wondrous mischief. While Descartes is questioning his own existence, suggesting that he may have been a dream or may not even have been born, the reader knows that Borges, inventor of Descartes, is raising these questions. He complicates the matter by affirming that the historical Descartes of the poem may also be an illusion, a dream. In sly metafiction comes the *other* Descartes. For Borges only that other Descartes, the doubter, the dreamer, the one outside the historical figure, exists. In typical reversal, the real one is merely illusion, but Borges's creation of an outside dreamer is real.

And what happens to the dreaming Descartes? Borges uses him in an extended metaphor to portray a dreamer of philosophers and gods and timeless beasts. Can we learn more about him? We want to. We must. But this other Borges will never be caught in an act of epiphany, spilling the truth. The artist as well as the philosopher Borges will not allow inept revelation. In his lifelong quest for the word, the key to the universe and its enigma, Borges never descends to explanation, to anticlimactic arrival. He will never reach and set anchor in Ithaca. He will not spoil the necessary mystery with pretensions of truth.

Although Borges will not spell out fixed verities, he acknowledges that not only his characters but he too has experienced what he cannot express: "In many cases, in the case of ecstasies, that can only be told through metaphors, it cannot be told directly. It has to be told through metaphors. That is the reason why the mystics always resort to the same metaphors. A metaphor may be conceptual or a mystic might talk in terms of the grape or the rose or also of fleshly love. Even the Persian mystics do, the Sufis" (Barnstone, *Borges at Eighty,* 168–69).

In his personal quest for salvation, Borges confesses that this experience of total otherness occurred twice in his life. I was talking to him about the mystical experience of Saint John of the Cross when he revealed, "In my life I only had two mystical experiences and I can't tell them because what happened is not to be put into words, since words, after all, stand for a shared experience. . . . Twice in my life I had a feeling. . . . It was astonishing, astounding. I was over-whelmed, taken aback. I had the feeling of living not in time but outside time. I don't know how long that feeling lasted, since I was outside time" (Barnstone, *Borges at Eighty,* 11).

In these two instants when Borges reaches into "the other time," the communication is poor between the ordinary and the extraor-dinary. The ineffable nature of mystical contemplation derives more from the absence of a clear memory in that altered state than from the lack of a proper descriptive lexicon to convey vision. Hence the notion of oblivion and ineffability associated with mystical transport.

Borges says that such a moment of ecstasy—when one is really elsewhere, in another time, another place, in another being; when one is the other—is not a shared experience. Dreams and any foray into the unconscious are rather hard to capture on cassette recorders. But he does find metaphors. His fascination with ecstasy and his discomfort with eternity he best expresses in a few lines of poetry. After going through dreams of ancient places and artworks that the New York Cloisters have brought to mind—the labyrinth at Knossos, Leif Ericsson's America, the white unicorn in its own halted time—he is weary and a bit skeptical of such ventures:

> Siento un poco de vértigo.
> No estoy acostumbrado a la eternidad.
>
> I feel a bit dizzy.
> I am not used to eternity.
> ("The Cloisters," *La cifra,* 32)

The speaker has brought us to the brink of a poetic intuition. Although it lies in that imminence of a revelation that does not come, he will explore the main conditions of the revelation: illusory time and discomforting eternity. Borges comes to the illusory nature of time through Berkeley, Hume, and Schopenhauer, but the roots both of time's annihilation and dizzying eternity are in Buddhism. Eternity, that is, the simultaneity of all time, slips into nothingness. And he uses Buddhist principles, such as those found in the fifth-century Buddhist treatise the *Visuddhimagga (Way of Purity),* to refute temporal succession, to refute ego, his own existence and that of the astronomical universe. In the *Way of Purity* temporal succession is reduced, as life itself is reduced, to an infinitesimally brief instant, as "a chariot wheel in rolling rolls only at one point of the tire, and in resting rests only at one point" (Radhakrishnan, *Indian Philosophy*, I, 373). Borges cites this Buddhist metaphor in his "New Refutation of Time." But in the end he returns from speculation and rhetoric to his irreversible destiny, which is to shun eternity and live in time. He confesses in the last lines of the same essay: "Time is the substance I am made of. Time is a river that carries me away, but I am the river. It is a tiger that destroys me, but I am the tiger; it is a fire that consumes me, but I am the fire. The world, unfortunately, is real. I, unfortunately, am Borges."

We are not unfortunate that, while he was flirting with the secular mystical, he reached for elusive intuitions in order to explore the oblivion outside time, only to return from his sojourn, albeit with a few illuminating metaphors and allegories; he returned to the diurnal duty of being himself, Borges, in the river, that destroying yet living river of time.

Perhaps the last Borges we must address is the first: Borges contemplating himself the writer, the voice talking aloud to us in his poems. He appears in the late poem "Aquel" (That One). He is a metafictional intruder in the text, like Unamuno in his novels. In the last line we witness the poet at work, yielding to his verses and, since crowds do not exist, speaking to each one of us personally.

After so many years, the poet is sick and tired of being himself, of looking at the public looking at him. However, it is his duty, given him by his father as a compensation for his military unfitness, to be a maker. He has been a maker now for six decades and has found neither the right words nor himself. But he knows very well the habits of that minor maker from the Southern Hemisphere. As always he is the best conspirator to spy on and denounce himself. Here is what he has to say about himself as "the other" in "That One" as he surrenders to his profession:

> O days consecrated to the useless
> task of forgetting the biography
> of a minor poet of the southern
> hemisphere, to whom fate and the stars
> gave a body leaving no son behind
> and blindness that is penumbra and prison,
> and old age, the dawn of death,

and fame, which no one deserves,
and the habit of contriving pentameters
and the ancient love of encyclopedias
and of fine calligraphic maps
and slender ivory and an incurable
nostalgia for Latin and fragmentary
memories of Edinburgh and Geneva
and the forgetting of dates and names
and the cult of the Orient, which peoples
of the miscellaneous Orient do not share,
and the vespers of tremulous hope
and the abuse of etymology
and the iron of Saxon syllables
and the moon, which always surprises us,
and that baleful custom, Buenos Aires,
and the taste of grapes and water
and cocoa, a Mexican sweetness,
and some coins and a sandclock
and one evening like so many others
on which he yields to these verses.

The Borges I knew was blind. Somehow he opened all the windows of the world to show the morning of his created light. Blindness was his midcareer gift, which ironically coincided with his being named director of the 800,000-book National Library. As did Milton in "On His Blindness," in his poem "In Praise of Shadow" the poet complains, conveying the urgency of his solitude and the need to fill it with his verse. But there is equal recognition of blindness as a real gift:

There were always too many things in my life;
Democritus of Abdera tore out his eyes in order to think;
time has been my Democritus.

This penumbra is slow and gives no pain;
it flows down a mild slope
and looks like eternity.

When Borges had eyes that saw, he often wrote about vague, blurred streets, mysterious red clouds, invisible presences. When his own eyes blurred, he put vagueness aside and gave us his clear vision of the present, a panorama of a real and imaginary historical past, and bequeathed us a sharp engraving of his several nights: the darkness before his dead eyes and the inner night of the labyrinth. In one of the last poems, "La cifra," he urges us, imperatively, to recognize the sweet habit of discovering the night:

> We live discovering and forgetting
> That sweet habit of the night.
> Look at it carefully. It might be the last.

In these lines about the blindman, I have done what I do not do afterward: develop a more analytical discourse about his life and poems. From now on the person of Borges takes over. The rest is memoir. Since Borges, in his most memorable words, repeats his obsessions, I several times show an event or his discussion in different contexts. To edit out the levels of the palimpsest would be less true to Borges. I have also let the nature of memory dictate the form of memoir, and so, in keeping with memory's tangents, I have not ordered what follows with strict chronological intent.

On an Ordinary Evening
in Buenos Aires

"You know, Dante was wrong about hell, wrong about the meaning of that inscription on the gate of the Inferno in the first lines of Canto 3: LASCIATE OGNI SPERANZA, VOI CH'ENTRATE (Abandon every hope, you who enter). Hell doesn't begin down there. There is no entry to the afterlife. Hell begins here, and here is where we should abandon all hope. Then we have the possibility, the hope, of some momentary happiness."

Borges waited behind the door, by the oil portrait of his mother. Dressed in his usual black suit, neat, one shoelace untied, he wobbled a bit without his cane. The darkness of his clothes contrasted with his pallor. His face, tilted sideways and upward, smiled like a child's, yet severely, and his blind eyes glowed. He took me by the arm and said, "Come, sit down on the couch," and I found myself guiding him, and guided by him, across the room to the couch under the window.

As I sat next to the bookcases of his library, I thought of the many Borgeses who were living in that apartment under the name and in the mind and body of Jorge Luis Borges. The library—in childhood, his notion of Paradise—contained his father's English books. His mother's bedroom up the hall was his Hispanic garden of sixteenth- and seventeenth-century conquistadores and of nineteenth-century colonels fighting on the plains of rival dictators. And there was Borges himself, dressed properly like a literary man, the son of a near-blind professor of psychology, earning his living from his pen. That pen was often elsewhere, not only in the library of Babylon or the walls and palace of Shih Huang Ti, but in the slums of that other Buenos Aires, his childhood Palermo, where the tango was born in the brothels and was danced in the streets by hoodlums, by two men clasping each other, in preparation for their sexual games inside. In Borges was the fantasy of the pedant and the knife-dueling outlaw, of the Kabbalah and the pampa. Each possessed him with equal force and precision.

On another day, after a trip to China, I gave Borges a knife I had picked up in the Philippines. I got it, along with brass gamelans, from Mindanao in the south. It was a curved Muslim knife in a scabbard, a handsome piece with cheap jewels and age. The knife, like the Philippines, symbolized several of his preoccupations: Asia, Islam, the Hispanic. But it was a knife, and so it was also Buenos Aires. When I handed it to him, here was the instrument of manhood that some "ordinary *criollo* hounded by justice" would carry as he tracked the hint of a guitar in a worn-out wind through hollow houses, seeking an enemy to whom his blade would bring silence. In that neighborhood of his childhood and later imagination, even the prickly pear was a sinister growth and seemed planted in nightmare soil.

Borges took the knife and removed it from its sheath. To the surprise of us all, this somewhat frail man of eighty grabbed it by the handle and thrust it upward.

"Do you know what this is?"

My Peruvian friend José Miguel Oviedo was sitting with us — we were in a glitzy restaurant — and Oviedo started to answer, smirking and not a little taken back, "I suppose . . ."

"It's the killer thrust, the real killer thrust!"

On this September afternoon in 1975, my first with Borges in his Buenos Aires apartment, the poet sat me down on the couch. South American spring drifted in through the window behind us. We were not in his memory of the slum barrios of his "endless, ecstatic tramp-ings," but next to his library, a wall of books, most of them nineteenth- and early twentieth-century volumes, for his reading and especially his rereading. "I've spent my life squatting next to bookshelves and tramping through books."

I said nothing, looking around while he turned his eyes to the rows of unseen titles.

He blurted out, implausibly, "Don't you agree that English has developed toward a monosyllabic language?"

"Chinese *is* essentially monosyllabic," I retorted, happy to talk about language, "but it is moving the other way now, toward polysyllabism, since science, modern bureaucracies, and Marxist ideology don't care for the nice plainness of one-syllable words."

"Take the word *laugh*," Borges said. "In Old English it had two

phonemes, *hlehhan* or *hliehhan,* and two in old High German, *lachen.*
Yet just one syllable in modern English. *Laugh.* It's remarkable, no?"

Being blind and accustomed to the unknown, Borges plunged into
talk about language and philosophy with no preliminary pleasantries
whatsoever. Why wait? Why waste time on nonsense when the fun
of encyclopedias and the unknown surrounds us? So on our first day
together in Buenos Aires, Borges ruminated, mocked his own talents
and worth; we argued and laughed like old conspirators, nonstop and
breathless, and planned further mischief and collaboration.

One darkening afternoon a few weeks later, Borges was especially
perky and full of allusions and adventures. He began to quiz me. On
this particular day I was meditative, maybe morose, not up to his
wit. Usually I kept up with his games, and if he indulged in false
modesty I could undo him by agreeing with his self-deprecation. He
loved banter.

"I'm not much of a writer, you know. No imagination," he said.
"I can't create characters. There's just one, me, and perhaps Funes,
and he's also me. Some people think I am a good writer; they're
wrong. But I can't help it if they're mistaken. They want to be
mistaken about me, although I don't know why, and I suppose I am
pleased by their error. But they are still incorrect in their judgment."

"You should keep the secret of your inferiority under your hat."

"I would, if I wore a hat. And I should wear a hat to cover my
half-bald head."

"And how about hiding your nose?"

"My nose. Oh, you've noticed that too. It's just a piece of flesh-
colored meat. Really an awful appendage."

"Quevedo would have been pleased to use it for a model for one
of his lampoons, for a vicious insult poem."

"You think my nose is worthy of Francisco de Quevedo's attention?"

"No. But maybe we can stick you in there with his prostitutes
and copulating priests, or with Góngora's big nose that Quevedo said
came from his 'being a rabbi of the Jews.' "

Then Borges recited the lines I alluded to:

> ¿Por que censuras tú la lengua griega
> siendo sólo rabí de la judía,
> cosa que tu nariz aun no lo niega?

Why do you censure the Greek tongue
When you are but a rabbi of the Jews,
A fact your nose cannot deny?

That Spanish Golden Age poet and picaresque novelist Francisco
de Quevedo, outrageous, misanthropic against all professions and peoples, masterful, profoundly metaphysical, pessimistic, furiously obscene and amusing, at once a cynic and hopeless lover, was in those
months the author I was reading most. He frequently needles his
rival, the almost surreal baroque poet Luis de Góngora, for being a
disguised Jew—an accusation that was more correctly applicable to
his fellow Golden Age writers Saint John of the Cross, Saint Teresa
de Jesus, and Fray Luis de Leon, all of Jewish convert background.

Borges moved a bit, sat very straight, and smiled, looking right at
me and through me to a space beyond. Then he began, almost
didactically, "Now, you know that Quevedo attacked Góngora's nose
because in that period of recent *conversos* (converts), of forced *conversos,* that was his way of accusing this Church prebendary of being
a Jew. He was trying to mock the poet, to dishonor the man by saying
he had the stain of Jewish blood in his veins. All my life I've tried
to be a Jew, to be worthy of being of the Kabbalah, of those who
added up the numbers of Genesis to find the Word, who saw the
Creation itself as a mere symbol of the Word existing before the
Creation and before time. And even if I hadn't tried to be a Jew, on
my mother's side I am Acevedo, a typical Judeo-Portuguese name
from Salonika, and I'm also from the port of Pago de los Arroyos,
where in 1728 a Catalan farmer, Don Pedro de Acevedo, landed in
Argentina. Years ago the journal *Crisol* wrote about my 'Jewish ancestry, maliciously hidden.' They accused me correctly. I am a Jew.
Maybe the inquisitors will find my ancestors among the tribes of the
bituminous Black Sea."

"Borges, I absolve you of being from the breed of Gentiles. I am
a Jew with a *converso* name, a plain nose, not quite small enough
to be Tartar but very ordinary and so unimposing as to pass Quevedo's
critical eye. So I fail as a Jew. I'm not the right stereotype, yet I still
feel close to your favorites, Spinoza, Heine, and Kafka. You and I,
we're both in the same bag. I remember very well your essay, 'I, a
Jew,' where you said that mythology comes from the past, not the
future, that the past is infinitely supple for invention, and—like the

Druzes, the moon, like death, like last week—can be enriched by ignorance."

"We are always inventing our past. What else can we do, since we are the sum of our past—half memory, half invention?" Then, changing tacks, "By the way, do you know how Uruguayan gauchos castrate bulls?"

"How Uruguayan gauchos castrate bulls?" I said, stumped.

"With their teeth!"

"You make me sick."

The old gentleman raised his leg and carefully placed it over his knee. "It makes you feel uncomfortable to talk about it, doesn't it? Come, have some tea. Oh, can you tell me the etymology of bonfire?"

"Is this another trap?"

"Bonfire, Scottish bonfires."

"I guess it comes from *bon feu,* good fire. French."

"No," he said, in triumph, "Middle English."

"I'm sorry. Then I don't have a clue."

"You were right about the fire, but it's not Norman fire. It's from *banefyre,* a Saxon bone fire. The shepherds stood around on the highlands and built bonfires from sheepbones and cowbones to keep themselves warm. Come, have some tea," he repeated.

Borges rose, fragile. He took my arm and we walked to the table, which was set with biscuits and a teapot in its cloth igloo. When we were seated he asked me to read two sonnets I had translated into English. Again he tilted his head sideways and upward, smiling a big toothy smile. At such moments his teeth seemed to replace his eyes.

"Read away," he said. I read "A Key in Salonika" aloud.

> Abarbanel, Farías or Pinedo,
> Hurled out of Spain in an unholy, sweep-
> ing persecution, even now they keep
> The doorkey of a house lost in Toledo.
> From hope and terror they at last are free
> And watch the key as afternoon disbands.
> Cast in its bronze are other days, far lands,
> A weary brilliance and calm agony.
> After its door was dust, the bronze became
> A cipher of diaspora and wind
> Like the other temple key someone flung high

Into the blue (when Roman soldiers came
And charged with dreadful fires and discipline)
And which a hand received into the sky.

"Here I am again with my Spanish Jews in the Eastern diaspora. My forefathers were called Pinedo and Acevedo. I suppose I am partly a Jew. We are all of us in the West Greeks and Hebrews. These two essential nations, Greece and Israel. Rome is but an aftermath—an extended one. As for these poems," he began, with characteristic humor, "which are not worth much in Spanish—they are merely old-fashioned sonnets—you have taken them and have turned them into good English sonnets. Is it the English language of Milton and Hopkins which is simply better for this kind of thing?"

His dead eyes glowed (to cite one of his poems) and his face was animated.

"You won't get a plugged nickel out of me for your flattery," I replied. "You're beefing me up so I can praise you when you get on one of your 'humble' *Now let's bash Borges the writer* trips."

"I see you're onto my tricks, but I *wish* I were putting you on. I know my own Spanish attempts all too well. I know the limitations of my plain sonnets with their ordinary speech. Lugones was baroque. I'm plain."

"Your ordinary sonnets should never have been printed, but I have something to say about them anyway."

"Well, speak away. I suppose you'll let me have it. I am all ears."

"Those strangely un-Spanish sonnets of yours are perfectly and traditionally Spanish, even though they're not in Petrarchan but Shakespearean stanzas. The lines are so enjambed that they read like overheard speech. And form is almost invisible. It disappears. It's sleight of hand. They're stories you tell in invisible sonnets. That's it. Now I've flattered *you* and I take it all back."

"Good sonnets should be invisible," he insisted. "All form should be felt but invisible. The fact is that I use only simple rhymes in Spanish, the obvious ones that everybody knows. Anyway, here in Argentina no one reads poetry, so I'm free to do what I want."

"You certainly are. You've done so much of what you want, and your own way, that no one knows quite who you are. I wonder sometimes: Are you the most modern and experimental or the most anachronistic of contemporary writers? Or both? Are you writing poetry or prose? In the preface to your *In Praise of Shadow,* you say you don't distinguish between them . . ."

"No," he interrupted," I don't distinguish between *my* poetry and fiction, but others may do so."

"But I think you do distinguish between your poems and prose. Not so much in form, but in voice. When you write poems you're not all those people in the stories and essays, all those remote Borgeses you can't keep track of; and I prefer that personal Borges in the poems, the one who is playing with history or time or who is singing portraits of Spinoza, Swedenborg, or yourself, with a pathos not often in your stories."

"Then you don't despise the poems?"

"Only most of the time."

"You mean there's something to them? Barnstone, maybe you've been carried away. Surely you are deceived. I can document all the things wrong with them. But deception isn't bad. Alonso Quijano was splendidly deceived, intentionally deceived throughout two long books. I'm fond of those two dreamers, Alonso Quijano and his translator, Miguel de Cervantes."

"Yes. I suppose I am deceived about your poems. They're probably just bare, ruined windmills. Lots of wind and no sails."

"My friends say the poems are not much good. They're being sincere, and they mean well. They want to help me. They say I should write more stories and not waste my time on those verses. However, I must tell you I think of myself first as a poet."

"You and Cervantes, both of you think yourselves first of all poets, but Miguel de Cervantes was really wrong, since he wasn't a remarkable poet. Remember how in the *Quijote* he mentions that long-winded pastoral of his, the *Galatea,* as one of those fantastic readings that addled the mind of Alonso Quijano?"

"The *Galatea* would addle my mind too if I had to read it," he smiled, shaking his head. "Cervantes was a tedious, conventional poet. But he wrote one book of the dreamer."

"You've become the dreamer, and you're not even mad."

"Dream has become my habit," he said solemnly. "I should say dream is my profession, and, yes, I suppose I am not mad. At least not in the admirable manner of Alonso Quijano. But why not be mad like Quijano, the true author of the *Quijote?* One could do worse than to be the noble, foolish character he became. Will you come with me to visit a friend at the *Nación?"*

Borges took my arm and we set out for the elevator, about ten steps from his door. We stepped inside the metal box, which accelerated to its full slow speed of stillness. The ride down was a transitory eternity in which only invisible space seemed to be moving. Finally we slowed again, were back in time, and soon out in the street and on the way to the offices of the *Nación,* a leading newspaper where he was taking a poem to the literary editor.

Guiding Jorge Luis Borges through the streets of Buenos Aires was dangerous, at least for me. Perhaps I was delinquent, for although I paid attention to where we were going, it wasn't easy. Borges didn't let our dialogue slow for a second, even when we were caught in the middle of a boisterous street, with fat *colectivos* (the Buenos Aires buses) plunging toward us. Borges was perfectly right about conversation and distracting forces. He had his mind on what's essential: the exchange of words, ideas, and feelings. The rest of the world he didn't see, or care to be aware of (except when he wanted to — and then his blindness was no impediment to seeing). Those other forces, he was confident, would take care of themselves. Except for his 1938 Christmas Eve accident on the stairway, which left him near death (and even that event led to the story "The South"), Borges was to pass his life immune from accident. Often I marveled at his luck, remembering how many precarious automobile rides he took, sitting in the death seat, never with a seat belt, including one night in Chicago with me when we were so lost in conversation that I was, I confess, thoroughly irresponsible about watching the road. No accident, but I wonder if I was less blind than he on that luminous evening.

Borges knew the streets very well, knowing when to step up or down. Beyond the six or eight inches of bad vision in his right eye there lay a larger circle of hazy yellow, the first color he remembered from childhood; in that yellow haze he could often make out crucial curbs and steps. Much of the pavement, however, was broken, and there were cracks every ten or fifteen feet. In a poem from *La rosa profunda,* entitled "The Blindman," he wrote one of the most profound meditations not only on pitfalls in the street but on the prisonlike dream that is the condition of the blindman's solitude, and how, through his verse, he maps the lines of that sunless world:

> The varied world is plundered. Gone the sweep
> Of faces (that are what they were before),
> The nearby streets, today remote. And more,
> The hollow blue that yesterday was deep.
> Left in the books is only what remains
> In memory—forms of forgetfulness
> Which keep the format yet undo the sense,
> Flashing mere titles. But the street contains
> Ambushing breaks and holes. And each step won
> May be a fall. I am the very slow
> Prisoner of a dreamlike time, with no
> Way left to mark his dawn or fading sun.
> It's night. No one is here. And with my verse
> I must work out my insipid universe.

"The sidewalks are broken like this country, like the Argentine republic," he said.

As we walked slowly along, people generally moved aside. Even five policemen who were peacocking down the center of the pavement hesitated a moment, wavered, then moved aside as we came near them. It was remarkable to see them yield to the old writer, who was officially in disgrace with their Peronist leaders. Every minute or so someone came up to Borges and shook his hand. He confided in me that he had hired all these well-wishers, that the same ones would keep coming around the block.

"I do what Perón did; he hired people to come to rallies and shout *Perón! Perón! Perón!*"

One older man took Borges's hand and said he was glad there was at least one Argentine who was always brave enough to speak out politically, even at risk of career and life. Borges turned to all these unknown and unseen faces with full attention and gave them his Fernandel smile, usually grabbing their hand with his two. He enjoyed the encounters and was never jaded or weary. I suspect that although he seemed to use every moment not given to friendship for the purpose of reading, thinking, or writing, he welcomed these interruptions, any unexpected interruption, and that his normal condition of blindness had something to do with his willingness to be drawn out of himself.

Even in the bookstore across from his apartment, the Librería de la Ciudad, where he often went to dictate fiction or poems to his German-Argentine friend, Anneliese Von der Lippen, in the midst of creating and dictating a poem he was constantly interrupted by passersby. People could see him from the street, sitting at the desk directly behind the wide window separating the store from the galería walkway. They would come into the store, seize his hand, saying, *"Hola, Borges, soy Eduardo"* (Hello, Borges, I am Eduardo). Borges always stopped writing, even in the middle of a word, and turning to them, asked how they were, what news? Or with his inimitable laugh that started someplace deep and concealed, maybe in his pockets, and came up with sonorous candor, drawing everyone into it, he'd return the greeting with something outlandish like, *"Hola, Eduardo, y yo soy Borges"* (Hello, Eduardo, and I am Borges). Why should only the sighted (before the blind) have the privilege of naming themselves publicly? Borges needed to say who he was too, even if his observed appearance had already given him away.

Then, almost in dream, he would pass directly back to his dictation, as if there had been no intrusion from that passing world. Even the smile that lingered as he turned would vanish as soon as he was back in his staring posture of creation. Borges liked to work in company, since he was, as he frequently declared, a lonely, isolated man. Put more positively, he thrived on companionship. And the bookstore as workplace also had a specific advantage over his apartment: no phone calls. The public interruptions could not disturb his concentration.

(The historian Jonathan Spence wrote much of his mammoth volume, *The Search for Modern China,* at the Naples Pizza Parlor in New Haven, Connecticut. No phone, no pressure from the waiter to hurry his coffees. Just a few friends to greet him. Both Spence and Borges found a crowded public place suitable for thinking and writing. What could be better than to be writing away in a fine bookshop in an Argentine *galería* or in a discreet pasta joint in the refined rustbelt of America?)

The bookstore was Borges's habitat, as was the library — the childhood library, then the small public library where he first found employment, and later the National Library where he reigned modestly in darkness. Perón removed the outspoken Borges from his first position. It was not much of a job, cataloging books in the basement of what he called "the sordid library"; though there, while he was playing truant, he wrote "The Lottery in Babylon," "Death and the Compass," and "The Circular Ruins." Critics generously endowed their mysterious ciphers with mystical significance, although these were simply his recordings of the number of books and shelves at his elbow.

The despair and boredom in the infinite library in "The Library of Babel" were in part from Kafka, who more than anyone else was to turn Borges during these years to the writing of short fiction. As for his misery, it was real. There is even a touch of tears and sentimentality, of rare self-pity, as Borges recounts this period in his "An Autobiographical Essay." (He wrote the essay in English, and it came out as a long afterword to *The Aleph and Other Stories*.) "Now and then during these years, we municipal workers were rewarded with gifts of a two-pound package of maté to take home. Sometimes in the evening, as I walked the ten blocks to the tramline, my eyes would be filled with tears. These small gifts from above always underlined my menial and dismal existence" ("An Autobiographical Essay," *The Aleph and Other Stories*, 242).

In 1946 he was fired from the Miguel Cané Municipal Library— or rather, promoted to a higher position, that of inspector of poultry and rabbits, in an attempt to humiliate the dissident intellectual. Borges truly believed that Perón was a Nazi and said so openly. In his "Autobiographical Essay" Borges explains, "I went to the City Hall to find out what it was all about. 'Look here,' I said. 'It's rather strange that among so many others in the library I should be singled out as worthy of this new position.' 'Well,' the clerk answered, 'you were on the side of the Allies—what do you expect?' His statement was unanswerable; the next day, I sent in my resignation" ("Essay," 244).

When Perón fell in September 1955, Borges's public nightmare ended. For his resistence to Perón, he was offered the position of director of the National Library. Borges viewed this as a great laughable honor, since by then he was nearly blind. Emir Rodríguez Monegal, Borges's friend, disciple, and intellectual biographer, masterfully and gracefully describes Borges's euphoria as he took him on a tour through his new symbol become real, his labyrinth:

Borges took me in hand and led me around, seeing only enough to know where each book he wanted was. He can open a book to the desired page and, without bothering to read—through a feat of memory comparable only to that of his fictional Irineo Funes—quote complete passages. He roams along corridors lined with books; he quickly turns corners and gets into passages which are truly invisible, mere cracks in the walls of books; he rushes down winding staircases which abruptly end in the dark. There is almost no light in the library's corridors and staircases. I try to follow him, tripping, blinder and more handicapped than Borges because my only guides are my eyes. In the dark of the library Borges finds his way with the precarious precision of a tightrope walker. Finally, I come to understand that the space in which we are momentarily inserted is not real; it is a space made of words, signs, symbols. It is another labyrinth. Borges drags me, makes me quickly descend the long, winding stair-case, fall exhausted into the center of darkness. Suddenly, there is light at the end of another corridor. Prosaic reality awaits me there. Next to Borges, who smiles like a child who has played a joke on a friend, I recover my eyesight, the real world of light and shadow, the conventions I am trained to recognize. But I come out of the experience like one who emerges from deep water or from a dream, shattered by the (other) reality of that labyrinth of paper. (Monegal, *Borges,* 430–31)

As we were strolling along those streets of Buenos Aires, sifting through the crowds, Borges talked about Paul Groussac, the former blind director of the National Library and the splendid irony that he, Borges, had become chief inspector and guardian of 800,000 books at the time when he was similarly granted darkness. All this he recorded in a major poem, with its mischievous title "Poem of the Gifts," dedicated to his friend and collaborator María Esther Vásquez. Here he describes his ancient paradise of gloom:

> Slow in my darkness, I am exploring the
> Thread of twilight with my faltering cane,
> I who imagined Paradise was the domain
> Under the heading of a library.
>
>   . . . now I look upon
> A dear world coming apart like smoldering trash,
> Formless, burning into a vague, pale ash
> That looks like sleep and like oblivion.

As we moved away from reflections on the library, Borges turned our talk to American and English poets. People in the street kept stopping us.

"You are immortal, Borges!" cried one woman to him.

"Thank you, but save me from such eternal condemnation," he said grimly. He had different answers for this frequent salutation, just as he had different answers for the question "How do you feel about the Nobel Prize?" My favorite reply, which was no turn of phrase, no escape or dismissal, consisted of one word. He uttered it in an auditorium at Indiana University.

"Greedy."

"Look here," he told me, "Eliot is a good poet, but a stuffy critic. Too professorial, no? But Robert Frost is a magnificent, yes, a very fine poet, like Browning. I hear he was a terrible farmer."

"Frost wrote in a simple language," I said, "a profoundly simple language, with all the multiple rooms of meaning of a William Blake. Most of his life they called Frost old fashioned and hokey, or he was simply ignored by 'serious' critics. Now he's redeemed and modern, with many levels of gloom, mystery, and confessional madness to his diction. He's aged very well."

On another occasion in his apartment, Borges spoke of being asked to meet John Kennedy. The appointment fell through but that didn't trouble him. He did mind, however, that he never spoke to the author of "I have been one acquainted with the night," with Robert Frost, whom he admired.

"You are acquainted with the night," I said.

"Mine is the history of the night," he answered.

A year later Borges was to publish his volume of poems entitled *Historia de la noche* (History of the Night).

Borges's constant enthusiasm for Frost was matched by his disdain for Ezra Pound, whose scholarship he thought ludicrous and his poetry not worth mentioning.

"I have one word for Ezra Pound. *Fraud.*"

While he could be wrongly ungenerous toward some contemporaries, particularly Lorca and Ortega, whose works he hardly knew, Pound he could not abide. For Pablo Neruda he had very different words. It wasn't clear to me whether he was praising Neruda for his weakest work as a way of undoing him, or whether he was giving the respected devil his due. Yet clearly he held him in esteem.

"Pablo Neruda wrote all those silly, sentimental love poems at the beginning, you know, *Veinte poemas de amor y una canción desesperada* (Twenty Love Poems and a Song of Despair), but when he became a Communist his poems grew very strong."

He did reproach Neruda for never saying a word against Perón when Perón was torturing Argentine Communists and sending them off to freeze in Patagonia. That was Communist party policy at the time, since the Argentine C.P. was wary of alienating workers, who despite their maltreatment were strongly allied with Perón. In a conversation about Neruda with Richard Burgin, Borges said, "When he was supposed to be writing at the top of his voice, full of noble indignation, he had not a word to say against Perón. And he was married to an Argentine lady; he knew that many of his friends had been sent to jail. He knew all about the state of our country. . . . But, of course, that doesn't mean anything against his poetry. Neruda is a very fine poet, a great poet in fact. And when that man [Miguel Angel Asturias] got the Nobel Prize I said it should have been given to Neruda" (Burgin, *Conversations*, 95–96).

Neruda was equally tactful and witty. About Borges, Neruda told Rita Guilbert in an interview: "He's a great writer and thank heaven for that! . . . But to quarrel with Borges, just because everyone wants to make me quarrel with Borges—that I'll never do. If he thinks like a dinosaur, that has nothing to do with my thinking. He doesn't understand a thing about what's happening in the modern world, and he thinks that I don't either. Therefore, we are in agreement" (Guilbert, *Seven Voices*, 30).

"By the way, have you read the poems of Robert Lowell?"

Borges stopped and turned to me. With his special enthusiasm, as if offering a secret to a private congregation, he declaimed, "No, I have not read the poems of Robert Lowell, and I think it is safe to say I will not read the poems of Robert Lowell."

"But what do you mean?"

"I mean that I have met the man, here in Buenos Aires. He came to my apartment. He brought me a book."

Borges's tone flowed from humor to mock gravity and then spread into scoffing indignation.

"Lowell and I chatted a while in the living room. He asked me about the pictures on the tables, the ones of my nineteenth-century family. Then, suddenly, this cousin of Amy Lowell lay down on the floor, took off his trousers and, wearing nothing but his undershorts, began to scream. I don't know what he said. I thought he was a madman. I assure you, he didn't act like a gentleman."

"Gentleman or madman, I bet you would feel a kinship, maybe a deep one, for his *Lord Weary's Castle.*"

"I've heard that this Lowell likes Hawthorne and I am also a nineteenth-century man. I made it by only one year, you know, born in 1899. I just sneaked into that century. Well, I might like his poems — but only if he keeps his trousers on. I would say that would be a condition."

"You are very demanding, Borges."

We talked about Yeats, who got better as he got older, and e e cummings, who did not, and Eliot, who stopped altogether. He praised Yeats for being a modern baroque poet, for his "gong-tormented sea," although (with Antonio Machado) Borges shared a disdain for the baroque, especially for the modern complication of it. He had no great love for William Butler Yeats, whom he unfairly placed between the arched sentimental and the baroque.

As for the much more baroque poetry of Gerard Manley Hopkins, he was in awe. I'll never forget the evening when I had been reading him favorite poets, Cavafy, Stevens, Frost. Then I turned to "The Wreck of the Deutschland," surely one of the most difficult poems in the English language. It is of the order of Sor Juana Inés de la Cruz's seventeenth-century "Primero sueño" (First Dream). Borges was entranced by the poem, which he had not heard before. A week later, on a Saturday morning, he quizzed me about lines he recited:

> Thou mastering me
> God! giver of breath and bread;
> World's strand, sway of the sea;
> Lord of living and dead;
> Thou hast bound bones and veins in me, fastened my flesh,
> And after it almost unmade, what with dread,
> Thy doing; and dost thou touch me afresh?
> Over again I feel thy finger and find thee.

"Who wrote those lines?"

I guessed a famous seventeenth-century English author, and I am embarrassed to say who it was; I should have known Milton's work better. (Yet I'd even taken my blue-cloth copy of Milton with me to

Argentina.) But I was too overwhelmed by his melodious recitation. Milton *should* have written it.

"You are a few centuries off. It's Hopkins. You read me the lines last week." He was very pleased to catch me.

I knew Borges didn't possess a copy of Hopkins in his library. He was enjoying his gnomic game. It was Funes again, the memory wizard, whose powers were out of control.

"Monster!" I said to him. I reserved that epithet for such extraordinary feats. "But how, after only one reading, can you remember those lines?"

"There are lines harder to forget than to remember."

All of Borges is my "habit," but of course his poetry is for me its center. I think of Borges's writing, in all genres, as moving toward simplicity. He himself often spoke of his early young man's "baroque" essay and fiction writing, rejecting it the way Pasternak rejected his early experiments or Robert Lowell later disparaged the obscurities of *Lord Weary's Castle.* And he never did permit the republication of those essays in the first edition of *Inquisiciones.* "Too clever and obscure for me to stomach," he would say. Yet each of these three authors is in part bluffing, for no writer like Lowell, Pasternak, or Borges rejects (except for *Inquisiciones*) some best-known works absolutely. "Apparent" rejection is necessary in order to go on, in order not to repeat oneself, to develop, to change, and not to fall into a mannerist imitation of oneself—as cummings did, as Jorge Guillén did, as even Frost did toward the end; but as Yeats, Cavafy, Aleixandre, and Rilke decidedly did not, much of their extraordinary new work coming fresh in their last years.

"Pound and cummings put their masks on when they write poems, but you take yours off," I commented.

"Listen, Barnstone, it's only reasonable. You know my tricks. Since I'm always playing Borges, the original but proper gentleman, I've got to put my madnesses and heresies someplace. So when I'm very upset I alter feelings a bit and store them in poems. Yet I should wear a mask in life, and not because of literary whimsy. I have looked at a mirror in my time, and I have a memory. I remember what I look like. That is why I should wear a mask."

"I agree."

"I *thank* you for being agreeable."

"Yes, cover your face, Borges, and make the world a prettier place."
"I'll send Fanny out tomorrow to pick me up some old rag or veil."

As for Borges's late poetry, it is the culmination of his career as a writer. He had not yet written in poetry the equivalent of his story "The Gospel According to Mark," but shortly before he died, in his most "uncovered" collection of poems, Borges found in the Greek Scriptures the pathos of ordinary suffering. He published "Christ on the Cross" in his last book, *The Conspirators* (1985). It is a major poem in the Spanish language. Ostensibly a portrait of the man Jesus, whose "black beard hangs over his chest," it is also the unmasking, the revelation, of a suffering Borges. In no early poem or fiction do we see such harsh vulnerability or plain, grim agony.

> Christ on the cross. His feet touch the earth.
> The three beams are the same height.
> Christ is not in the middle. He's the third one.
> His black beard hangs over his chest.
> His face is not the face of engravings.
> He is harsh and Jewish. I don't see him
> and will go on seeking him until the last
> day of my steps on the earth.
> The broken man suffers and is quiet.
> The crown of thorns cuts him.
> He is not reached by jeers of the mob
> which has seen his agony so many times.
> His or another's. It's all the same.
> Christ on the cross. Confusedly
> he thinks of the realm that maybe awaits him,
> thinks of a woman who was not his.
> It's not given to him to see the theology,
> the indecipherable Trinity, the Gnostics,
> the cathedrals, Occam's knife,
> the purple, the miter, the liturgy,
> the conversion of Guthrum by the sword,
> the Inquisition, the blood of the martyrs,
> the atrocious Crusades, Joan of Arc,
> the Vatican that blesses armies.
> He knows he is not a god and is a man
> who dies with the day. It doesn't bother him.

What bothers him is the hard iron of the nails.
He's not a Roman. He's not a Greek. He moans.
He has left us splendid metaphors
and a doctrine of pardon that can
annul the past. (That sentence
an Irishman wrote in a jail.)
The soul seeks its end, hurriedly.
It's darkened a bit. Now he is dead.
A fly walks quietly across the flesh.
What good does it do me that that man
has suffered, when I suffer now?
                                        Kyoto, 1984

Borges has committed hubris, using the metaphor of Christ to show his own suffering. And like Sappho, who inserts herself by name into poems in conversations with Aphrodite ("yet Sappho/I loved you"), Borges compares himself to a harsh black-bearded Jew, a man, not a mythical god, though others will later call him the Christian Godman Jesus. He compares his own hurt to that of Jesus, with no shame, with no false modesty or arrogance, but perfectly naturally.

Borges's last years were happier than others in his life. Or they seemed so. I find strident contradictions, however, between this popular image and the persona in his late work. To put it simply, Borges's early life as a writer in Argentina was often not easy. There was the dismal library job, the many years when he was writing work that was gaining him world recognition while holding down what he considered a demeaning position—the plight of a "nonprofessional" from an old family of prestige that had lost its fortune and power. Liberation from the municipal library came only when he was to suffer the first years of the Perón dictatorship. Yet during this period the speaker in his work is not grave; it is not remarkably personal at all. In later years, however, when he was apparently more peaceful, even joyful, culminating with his marriage to María Kodama, he wrote his most intensely personal, his darkest, his most despairing poems. And his best.

Truly there is a contradiction—as there should be.

Our walk went on, and our relentless chatter. A lady approached and rather hysterically called Borges Argentina's greatest writer. (Not an unreasonable judgment.) He took her hand and, not without amused irony, answered gently, "My dear friend, what you have said is clear proof that our country is going through a great trial."

Upon reaching the Nación building, we had to walk up broad marble stairs to the office. We mounted three flights, the design engineered for modest pomp and glory, not comfort. It was not easy, but Borges did not want to rest.

"If I rested, I might get tired. You know, at my age I had better conserve my strength and not rest."

In the office of the literary editor, Jorge Cruz, Borges carefully slipped a poem out of his suitcoat inner pocket. He put it on the editor's desk. Borges was pleased, familiar, yet outwardly diffident. Cruz read out loud "The White Deer":

> From what old border ballad out of green
> England, what Persian print and what arcane
> Regions of days and nights that still contain
> Our past, emerged the white deer through the scene
> I dreamt this morning? In a flash. I saw
> It cross the meadow, lose itself in gold
> Of an illusory day: lithe creature mold-
> ed from a bit of memory and the draw
> Of oblivion—a deer on one side only then.
> The gods who guard this strange world let me dream
> Of you but not control you. Maybe in a seam
> Of the deep future I'll find you again.
> White deer of dream, I too am dream in flight,
> Lasting no more than dream of fields and light.

"Do you like it?" Borges asked.

"It will do," Cruz answered, deadpan.

"You mean you don't really care for it?" Borges said, downcast.

"It will do."

Borges was genuinely pleased. "You're teasing an old man, no?"

"How did you guess?" Cruz said. "Moreover, how dare you imagine I am not merciful about every poem you offer us?"

Borges liked to invite derision in which he was the object. He never stopped playing his games of modesty, fame, outrage, time, the fantastic, metaphysics, death.

"Cruz is a charitable chap," Borges confided to me as we left. We walked a few steps. He turned.

"You know, Barnstone, I don't feel that I wrote that poem."

"What do you mean?"

"I mean I physically dictated the words. But I didn't make them up. The poem was given to me, in a dream, some minutes before dawn. At times dreams are painful and tedious, and I object to their outrage and say, enough, this is only a dream, stop. But this time it was an oral picture that I saw and heard. I simply copied it, exactly as it was given to me."

"You copied it. I think the best things we do are when we yield to what's there," I blurted, "when we don't combine or invent but yield to the obvious vision that is present or imminent, and we're willing to uncover it, to see it, copy it. In the introduction to the *Vita Nuova,* if I remember rightly, Dante copies from his book of memory. He is a scribe of hidden memory."

"Yes, but Dante worked perhaps not so much to retrieve the memory as to furnish that memory with its experience. My dream was there, one sided, in a flash, in the morning as I was waking."

"You were cunning enough to receive the dream, as it was, and be its scribe."

"I was cunning enough."

Borges normally published all his poems first in *La Nación.* This custom of newspaper publication still persists in Argentina. Years earlier Borges published with another leading paper, but when they turned him down he switched. He never forgot the slight. During the Dirty War, when Borges became convinced of what the military was up to, he ceased to publish in *La Nación,* since the paper supported the military government. And then Borges denounced the government and for the first time even spoke against his own military ancestors. He had always romanticized and heroized them, including his paternal grandfather, Colonel Francisco Borges (husband of his English grandmother) who, after the battle was lost, mounted his white horse and rode into enemy lines until the Remington cracked and felled him.

Borges's conviction about the diseased minds and malignant be-havior of the military was reinforced when, after the generals fell, he went to the public hearings in which details of torture (much of it sexually sadistic) and execution were recounted. Horrified, he made further declarations. But to many of his critics, Borges's understand-ing—as well as that of many "respectable" citizens, including the director of *La Nación*—came late, much too late. Too late to influence—if influence were possible—the policy of those unmusical generals, Videla and Viola.

The main impediment to Borges's early understanding was that this same military had thrown out Isabelita Perón on March 24, 1976, and anyone throwing out a Perón had to be good. (An enemy of my enemy is a friend.) Such was the case with the first expulsion of Juan Perón by Admiral Isaac Rojas, who actually restored democracy for a while. Initially virtually everyone, including Perónists, welcomed the expulsion of Isabelita; I was there and remember very clearly. But it was also soon luridly clear that the death squad thugs who worked in the AAA for López Rega under the Peróns were continuing their work of kidnapping and murder under the generals, with increased vengeance, tempo, and number of victims, and now not only against the military opposition but against any opposition, actual or perceived: against students, intellectuals, Jews, journalists, and their relatives and friends. When the director of *La Nación* found that his own daughter was a "disappeared" victim of the death squads, the newspaper ceased to support the military.

As we descended the three flights, Borges found it difficult. There was no handrail and the steps were steep. As he leaned on me he said, "You know, Dante was wrong about hell, wrong about the meaning of that inscription on the gate of the Inferno in the first lines of Canto 3: LASCIATE OGNI SPERANZA, VOI CH'ENTRATE (Abandon every hope, you who enter). Hell doesn't begin down there. There is no entry to the afterlife. Hell begins here, and here is where we should abandon all hope. Then we have the possibility, the hope, of some momentary happiness."

By now we were strolling down Florida, my favorite street in South America, closed off to traffic like the Calle de las Sierpes in Seville or similar mosaic-pebbled walkfares in Portugal. Borges was talking about one of his favorite poets, Emily Dickinson, with whom he shared metaphysical and introspective territories.

"Dickinson comes right out of Emerson, don't you think? I mean she has the rebellious spirit of Brahman New England which Emerson, that neglected intellectual poet, stands for."

With the mention of each poet he would recite a stanza or two of a poem; he read them from his memory notebook. "To Norway, to Norway, to Norway o'er the foam," he intoned, with heavy Gaelic slurs. Then it was Browning, Heine, Anglo-Saxon.

We had now been walking for hours. Walking, talking, or, to phrase it in Borges's word, "living, wouldn't you say?" The streets of Buenos Aires gave him the opportunity to live with his talking friends, to talk with his companions, to discover the familiar buildings, walls, stores, and skies that he saw just as vividly with blind eyes as he had when his eyes were filled with ordinary photography. Of course he loved his travels abroad, and a walk in Iceland or a slow ride across the Brooklyn Bridge (Hart Crane's bridge, he called it) or the streets of Geneva or Cambridge were endlessly fascinating. Yet inevitably (except in his final exile, when he became his Geneva double) he returned in feelings and in fact to his *fervor de Buenos Aires*:

> New England, 1967
> It is the forms in dream that seem to change;
> Everywhere I see a slanting red house,
> A foliage with leaves of slender bronze,
> The winter chaste, firelogs piously strange.
> As on the seventh day, the earth is good.
> In twilight there is something that persists,
> Something that almost isn't: daring, sad,
> An ancient ring of Bible and the mists
> Of war. Soon (we are told) will come the snow.
> America at every corner waits
> For me, but in the sinking afternoon
> I feel the past so brief, the now so slow.
> Buenos Aires, I'm walking through your streets.
> I go on without why or when, but soon.

As we neared his house, I asked him how the poems came. We had just been speaking about the Parsis, those Zoroastrians who came as religious refugees to India from Muslim Persia in the seventh and eighth centuries. I asked him whether his poems ambushed him or swooped down on him like the vultures attacking the Parsi towers of silence.

"No, I walk around with them until they overpower me. Then I dictate them, because I can't keep them in the dark anymore."

"Why not?"

"Because since I am blind, I have lost the vision of darkness. I don't know what night is, since everything is a greenish blue or yellowish mist. And though it's too dark for the poems, it's never really dark enough in my head. I miss the dark, the total shadow."

"And when you dream?"

"I dream in all colors. And very intense colors, mind you."

"Do you dream in Old English?"

"Look here, I'm fond of Old English. I remember a few lines — there aren't that many lines to remember. Yet I don't know it that well, that is, to be able to dream in the language. I do dream of figures who came from that period. And I have been haunted by vague kings, you know, those early Hamlet ghosts from Scandinavia, and the other night it was Brunanburh. I was there, or suppose I was. I was the warrior at Brunanburh in A.D. 937."

Nobody at your side.
Last night I killed a man in the battle.
He was courageous and tall, from the bright stock of Anlaf.
The sword entered his chest, a little to the left.
He rolled on the ground and was a thing.
A thing that crows.
You will wait for him in vain, woman I haven't seen.
The ships that fled over the yellow water
Will not return him.
At the hour of dawn
Your hand will search for him out of dream.
Your bed is cold.
Last night I killed a man in Brunanburh.

"That was another poem you copied."

"So it was."

" 'The ships that fled over the yellow water/Will not return him.' Did you copy out a poem or a prose narration — I don't know which, if there is a which?"

"There's no which, no difference. It's a tight poem, but different from prose only by its line breaks, by its typography."

We slowed. Borges began to fish in his pocket for his keys.

"Look here, Willis, we're walking in the street, we're almost at my place, and I have had the impression that we were not dodging traffic, not surrounded by hurrying pedestrians but sitting in the living room, pulling out books, and arguing away."

"You are a very distracting man."

Several hours had passed. Borges was leaving that evening for America, where he would stay five days. When the car came to take us to the airport, the driver said his orders called for him to pick up a Mr. Bones. Borges thought the misspelling amusing but lugubrious.

"A few days ago, I took a cab to EMECE to speak to your editor Carlos Frías, and the driver, an educated fellow, informed me authoritatively that you, Borges, are an excellent short story writer, but he doesn't care at all for your novels. He said they lack social reality. He was very stern about it."

"Indeed they do. Yes, all those novels I have never written lack reality. And if I had actually written one, it would surely suffer a worse disease."

"We can safely say you are undistinguished as a novelist."

"Invisible."

"I'd say that's an extremist view."

"I go in for absolutes."

"And what do you think of our cab driver critic?" I asked, in the same spirit.

"Obviously the man has good taste, and we have similar literary judgments," Borges insisted. "Instinctively, he shares my fears about the novel, and he has used you as the messenger to warn me. You know it is not that I reject the novel—how can I reject the novel about the whale or Jim or even Alyosha?—but I reject myself and the novel. The truth is that I don't know whether I have the imagination to create other characters, whether I have the breath. My father did, and some day I will finish and publish the novel he left almost finished, which is a very good book.

"Now as for these people who have things to say about my work, I always feel regret when I hear their criticism, for I wish the person had come to me directly. I could have been loyally behind them. Of course, most of the time I am spared a knowledge of other people's wisdom, since I have never read any articles or books about myself; or I should say I did so once, the first book, many years ago, and have not repeated that mistake. If books about me come to the door, I give them away immediately, as I do any copy of any work that I have written. I'm happy to say that I don't possess a single copy of any book I've written.

"But yes, when somehow I hear about those people who disapprove of my work, I do wish that they had contacted me first. They have lost a fine opportunity to get Borges. They've lost a sincere friend with whom they might chuckle at his faults and his posturing. I'd be on their side. I don't care much for Borges either, and I care especially little about his work. There's much too much of it, and I don't reread it, though I believe very deeply in rereading others. At my age I read few new books, but I am always rereading.

"As for that bothersome writer Borges, I have an advantage in being able to hit his weaknesses, his blunders, his shoddy scholarship, his pretensions about good writing, since I know some secrets about the work and my antagonist and I could — and should — get together and really do him in. I would enjoy that. But then my secrets aren't worth much, whatever I pretend, since you know that an author only initiates the process; the intentions are soon lost, and should be, and the rest is you. By the way, the 'you' stands for the reader, whom I can only think of — if I do so at all — as a single reader. The notion of readers plural, of an author talking to readers, doesn't exist — and if it does, it should not."

We climbed into the car. Borges knew when to duck to avoid hitting his head. He and I sat in the back seat, María in front with the driver. As we moved toward the airport, his mood was grave. He spoke about his mother, whose recent death, in July 1975, was constantly with him.

"She was ninety-nine when she died a few months ago," he said. "She suffered for two years and so much the last six months that each night she used to pray for that night to be her last. And when she woke up in the morning and found herself alive she said that God must be punishing her for some sin she could not remember."

"Like your story of those hundred- and two-hundred-year-old patriarchs condemned to the fate of living, unable to die."

"Yes. But when I wrote that story I was quite happy, you know. I was spoofing, really making fun of old age and the notion of earthly immortality and the dilemma of Tithonos. I never dreamed it would really happen to us."

"And your own death?"

"It may come like a black bird in the night. I won't care. Although I tell others that I am weary, sick and tired of the loneliness of being Borges each day, I do have poems to write, books to write, places to see."

"The Orient?"

"I haven't even been in the Near Orient, which, from a European point of view, we arrogantly call the Near East. I suppose for the Japanese California is the Far East."

"You would like the Altar of Heaven in Peking. You've already gone to the Great Wall with the Yellow Emperor. Why do you keep company with famous book burners?" I asked him accusingly. If I hit him with some personal or literary sin, it always perked him up.

"Look here, I am innocent," he whispered. "I am also innocent about my knife fighters and North European confidence men. Or am I?"

"Why, they burned Bruno and William Tyndale at the stake for much less than you have said. Compared to them you are a real heresiarch."

"Do you think I have chance of being so honored?"

"Your new book, *La rosa profunda,* is obsessed with blindness."

"Yes, it is an obsessed book. But I don't speak about blindness in order to complain. I am simply telling people something I know about, what it is like to be blind."

"Has blindness affected your other senses?"

"Perhaps my memory's a little better. It has to be, since all the time I have to remember things, to look things up in my memory. I'm afraid I've turned my head into its own library. You know I have to keep many things in my mind. Perhaps that is why I keep returning to familiar themes. I remember quotations and, like Samuel Johnson, am in danger of becoming a quotation of a quotation."

"An allusion of an allusion. Your Chinese background."

"No, an illusion of an illusion — Plotinus."

"Now you're going to a conference and they're going to talk about you. I know you don't read books about yourself. How is it that you're willing to hear people talk about you?"

"Things like this always happen, because I think *No* and always say *Yes.* I don't know why I am getting on a plane."

We were climbing the steps to the plane. María was ahead of us and entered the cabin. There was a particularly difficult part of the metal ramp. "Where am I?" Borges inquired.

"About one foot ahead you must step up, walk a step, and you will be inside."

He moved his cane back and forth. Then, as sometimes I saw him get out of a car on the wrong side and dangerously but imperturbably shuffle to the curb before someone caught up with him, he plunged ahead. His mind was on the steps and also elsewhere, for at the top of the ramp he stopped. For about a minute, for no obvious reason, he raised his eyes and looked toward what he might have thought was the night sky; he was actually staring at the side of the plane, a few feet above his head. It was an interminable wait for everyone following, who also obediently stopped. No one moved or talked or attempted to move him on. Borges stared, smiled, stared. Then he looked down and, after dutifully gauging the distance with his cane, stepped carefully into the cabin.

The Old English Lesson

Once, at supper in Chicago, he showed me and had me feel the deep dent in his forehead at the hairline where he had bumped his head.

"What did you do when you came to?"

"Why, I took out my gold watch, looked at it, and, seeing that it was working, I said to myself, 'I must be alive.'"

In my apartment on Paraguay Street, just a block up from La Plaza de San Martín where Borges lives, I'm scribbling on the floor amid my usual mess. Last night I worked through the night. It's a translation of "Spinoza," a sonnet on the old Jew polishing his lenses in the Dutch ghetto, whose walls and gardens smell of hyacinths and endless afternoons. I am careful, even nervous, to make the rhymes full, not half-rhymes. Once, after we had gone over a poem, Borges discreetly sent his editor, Carlos Frías, to tell me that the off rhymes I was mixing in weren't right. He wanted an exact rhyme, *rima consonante.*

I was defensive, saying Emily Dickinson invented slant rhymes, Wilfred Owen used them. Borges doesn't quite realize that nowadays in English off rhymes are more common than . . .

"Try a little harder," Frías interrupted, which is what he said Borges had told him to tell me.

I am a little nervous, as always when doing versions of Borges's poems. At the same time I'm always eager to look (through his poems and prose) for the first time into the unrecognized system of Basilides, the accursed Gnostic, at his 365 levels of heaven, at their vertiginous towers and proliferation of angels. Such is the laboratory where Borges works, in Alexandria or Buenos Aires, the poor man on Earth caught in his own planetary shadow under the monumental and impassioned sky. And here this fabricator, the ultimate heresiarch, strings his verbs and nouns together, fashioning simulacra and absolving us of God and eternity.

The phone rings. I knock over the coffee. It's Borges, upset.

"Can you come right away?"

"Yes."

"Well, as you say, step on the gas," he pronounces with firmness and roguish delight. Borges likes American slang but is sometimes apologetic when he thinks he may be misusing it. I was sometimes apologetic too, as when he asked me to recite the words of "Frankie and Johnny" and I couldn't get beyond "Frankie and Johnny were lovers."

"What's up?" I said.

"It's those lectures I have to give in Michigan. I cannot possibly give ten. It's too many. You know, I don't think I'm up to it."

"Let's get you down some. Five is better, no? I'm on my way."

It's Sunday afternoon as I walk toward San Martín and Borges's flat. Despite the Dirty War, this is a city of walkers; whether at four in the afternoon or four or in predawn dimness, there is hardly a deserted street in this capital, and cafés and kiosks are open to serve the pedestrians. On my all too frequent all-nighters, I like to take a book or some work with me to a local café bar and spend an hour or two there, reading and scribbling. Especially in those hours one is likely to hear a bomb go off, blasting an apartment or a business, whose drama and details I will read about the next morning. It is also my habit to study the papers, so urgently filled with death and expectation, while taking breakfast coffee at one of the cafés along Paraguay or Corrientes. But now I'm winding through crowds on the narrow pavements of this downtown neighborhood. The cold and damp of August are gone, and in November I'm breathing in the bright spring air with its odor of street flowers, tobacco, and *colectivo* fumes as I reach 997 Maipú Street and turn in the iron gateway of Borges's respectable apartment building.

How many times I recall Borges fumbling with his keys late at night to open the black gate after some very long walk through the city. After writing, first among Borges's pleasures is friendship, and strolling and talking with a friend is its most intimate expression. As for the keys, there are real keys to gain access to a building, but his other keys are the algebra, the word, the missing letter, "the mysterious key to all his years" that his ancestor Francisco de Laprida is to discover in 1829 when the intimate knife rips across his throat and Laprida is killed by a band of gauchos under orders from the dictator Rosas, the Jaguar of the Plains.

And Borges thinks himself a key that one day will slip inside and turn the lock. In a few months he will record this metaphor in Michigan, in the sonnet "A Key in East Lansing":

> I am a key whose steel has been filed out.
> My crooked age was not cut aimlessly.
> I sleep vague sleep in channels I don't see
> In which I am a captive held throughout
> By keys. A sure lock waits for me within.
> It is unique, its door made of forged steel
> And tight glass. Inside, ready to reveal
> Itself, is the true hidden house. Deep in
> The scanty twilight, uninhabited
> A mirror glares into the nights and days
> And glares upon the photos of the dead,
> The tenuous past of photos. In this maze
> One day I will push up against the rock-
> Hard door, and slip inside to turn the lock.

Climbing the circular stairs, I also think of Borges one evening in the '30s, on Christmas Eve 1938, to be exact, when he was running up a stairway and suddenly felt something brush his scalp. He had knocked his head against a casement window. Pieces of glass stuck in his scalp. For him stairs are always an excuse to speak of Dante and dropping into the Inferno. When he fell to the floor on that historic afternoon, he wasn't sure where he was. His wound became poisoned with septicemia and for a month he hovered between life and death in the hospital. Once, at supper in Chicago, he showed me and had me feel the deep dent in his forehead at the hairline where he had bumped his head.

"What did you do when you came to?"

"Why, I took out my gold watch, looked at it, and, seeing that it was working, I said to myself, 'I must be alive.'"

Borges was taken to a hospital, where the wound was not properly disinfected before being sutured. He was unconscious for days, was operated on in the middle of the night. When he woke he began, for the first time seriously, to write fiction. Before that it was poetry and essays but no *ficciones*. The story "The South," with its dream levels of a medical operation and cutting scalpel, its Juan Dahlmann, ranch owner of Argentine military and Germanic ancestry and his uncertain knife fight, and Borges, the ubiquitous narrator, eventually emerged from that hospital experience. The very first action of "The South" involves Dahlmann acquiring a copy of *The Thousand and One Nights* (not an unlikely book for a Borges double), rushing up the darkened stairs and brushing his head perhaps against a bird or a bat. His ghastly wound is caused because a door (not a window, as in Borges's real experience) had been left open onto the stairway. Dahlmann is taken forcibly to a sanitarium, where a surgeon saves him from death from septicemia. There follow the details of the train ride south through the pampas, the meal in the general store, the challenge from the gaucho with hints of Chinese blood, and the naked dagger in his hand as he goes out the door to escape, to dream his double encounter with gaucho or surgeon, to fight and die liberated on the plain under the open sky. In that early story of the pampas— or was it in the sanitarium?—the precious elements of Borges's thought and style are visible: the book, the knife, the sumptuous joy of story and of action, the choice of knowledge through letters or a military action terminating with the unknown message of impending death.

Borges is at the door when I climb up to Apartment 6B. Without his cane, he is leaning distinctly to one side, standing (as E. M. Forster said of Constantine Cavafy) at a slight angle to the universe. He has his suitcoat off and stands pale, tottering a bit, in his very white shirt. His smile is huge.

"*Hola.*"

He leads me to the table, although, as always, I am also leading him. We sit and begin to go over a list of new titles for those Michigan *charlas.* Fanny, his Guaraní servant, brings us tea and crackers, which we down eagerly. Because of his blindness, it isn't easy for Borges to eat the main course, but he seems to enjoy the small tasks of taking tea and refreshments, which he can handle nonchalantly. He is always a gentleman, with the same dignity, whether foundering on steak and vegetables, or chatting in his deep, resonant voice in Spanish, French, German, or English on stage before thousands, or reciting a sonnet about Juan Muraña, his favorite Argentine *guapo* con man and knife fighter. What Borges truly enjoys at this table is his breakfast of dry corn flakes, which he considers his special culinary discovery from North America.

As we get down to work I find myself embarrassed, since I'm not sure of the spelling of several words, but Borges, though he likes to play, limits himself to a few helpful teasing suggestions on how I might remember how to spell Emanuel Svedberg (whom I knew only by his later popular name, Swedenborg).

Slowly we work out five good titles for the talks. At one point we drift into conversation about women. Over the past few months Borges has liked to talk to me about women he once knew or knows now. I can't say why. He has had many women friends, all literary, according to his biographer Emir Rodríguez Monegal, except for one or two youthful visits to the house of Geneva prostitutes—the "respectable" initiation to sexuality for young men of his generation. The literary women have been coauthors of books, travel companions, readers and scribes for his work: sister figures including his sister, Norah; mother figures including his mother, Leonor, who was for much of his life his closest companion and with whom he lived for thirty years in this apartment until her death at age ninety-nine. An almost marriage to his much younger literary collaborator María Esther Vázquez was halted by Leonor; and there was the brief, unreal "rebound" marriage to Elsa Astete Millán in 1967, forty years after their original short courtship. Monegal comments in *Jorge Luis Borges*: "Many years later, Borges broke his rule of silence and confided to María Esther Vázquez that one of the things he found strange in Elsa was that she did not dream. Being a dreamer himself, he must have discovered that Elsa's incapacity to dream kept them hopelessly apart" (472).

Borges's women, if Monegal and others are right, were not lovers, nor did he have, with the exception of María Esther Vázquez, any very deep or extended love relationships. When I have eaten with Borges together with María Esther (of course, after his divorce from Elsa), it has always been at Maxim's, and Borges remains especially solicitous and fond of his friend and former fiancée. Yet for all the limitations in his rapport with them, Borges loves women, loves to be with them constantly, to work alone with them, to share their confidence, and (as with men) their friendship.

One cannot go further in observing his life, and certainly not in his writing, to wish into existence love episodes. Borges is a private person and holds the keys to his proper existence. All this is not to suggest that he has not had flirtations, infatuations. How could he not? In his early eighties he is for a while obsessed with a young cashier at the Librería de la Ciudad, who finds immediate enemies among his then protectors, Fanny, Anneliese, and of course María Kodama. In the end, María will alter all the generalizations of his affective life with women. She will be the summation and fulfillment of the discovery of love.

Now Borges is telling me that long ago he did indeed admire Susana Bombal. He suggests I go to his bedroom to look at the picture on the dresser. There I'll find a framed photo of a Chilean novelist of the fantastic whom he had published in the magazine *Sur* at least three decades earlier. "A very handsome woman," he remarks.

I go down the dark hallway to the two bedrooms. The large, airy one at the end, with its almost bridal appearance, is where his mother had slept until she died only a few months earlier. This room remains uninhabited. After her death he felt again like the failure he often complained of being. He could not be happy. Yet, ironically, just then he was becoming increasingly fulfilled as a writer, the public man who is, as in his famous *Borges and I,* thoroughly confused with the personality of the brooding private person.

So we have Borges the figure of paradox, of contradictions. As a private man he lives alone, enjoys his meditations and "habits," and claims to disregard or welcome death, which will relieve him from both life and afterlife. His fear is that the afterlife may be real, which would be eternal torment, since it would be more of the same, and he's had enough. Yet no sooner does he reflect on torment and nightmare than he decides stoically to sit it out. He escapes to peace, even to the felicity of reflection and creation. There is no way that this private Borges, who claims dream as his normal condition and nightmare as his sleep, who sometimes glorifies soldier ancestors while deriding his nation's military, can be other than a mixed soul. The public writer works in the privacy of inspiration, and in isolation ponders fantastically, reasons philosophically, and falls into personal misery.

The sonnet "Remordimiento" (Remorse), which he wrote for his mother soon after her death, reflects the months when he could not escape the despairing Borges. He describes a figure who gave his "mind to the stubbornness of art," yet who has committed the worst sin a man can commit: unhappiness. The poem concludes, confirming his remorse,

> It never leaves my side, since I began:
> The shadow of having been a brooding man.

I step into his mother's room, which has not been used since her death. It is sunlit and cheerful. In its center is Leonor's bed, standing high and white with its own loquacious personality. The window looks out upon nineteenth-century neo-Gothic buildings. The luminous spring burns on this frozen time-capsule at the bottom of the globe, isolated from its European source, preserving an Anglo-French architecture for this population of early Spaniards and more recent Italians. There are no traces of the ancient New World, however; no lines from Indian pre-Columbian structures. That civilization has disappeared (or is not acknowledged); many Argentines would say that the real Indian culture was, after all, up north, in Peru and Meso-America. Argentina's capital is very superficially Spanish colonial, in contrast to the strong Spanish renaissance and baroque structures of Mexico City or Cuzco or Quito. In the capital of the republic of the pampas, nineteenth-century Anglo-French and European architectural forms dominate. If Buenos Aires lacks the equivalent of the old pastel-colored barrios where Quevedo, Cervantes, and Lope de Vega lived and wrote and which still contain their original apartments, brass plaques, and ambience, it does possess the noisy energy of Madrid's Gran Vía and its official buxom stone buildings with nubile facing, all emblematic of a nineteenth-century state where pompous progress and politics reigned.

Part of the city is also La Recoleta Cemetery, gaudy, neo-baroque, worthy of Paris. Borges hates it, although once, in the first volume of poems, *Fervor of Buenos Aires,* he wrote a moving meditation on "its rhetoric of shadow and marble," on its error and confusion of peace and death. When I mentioned one evening that I had spent the afternoon there, he was strangely disturbed and spoke of "that place of bad taste his conquistador and military ancestors were given for their burial place in *el lugar de mi ceniza*" (the place of my ashes). His response to the cemetery, which still allured him enough to cause him to revile its nature, was almost violent.

"La Recoleta. What a terrible, morbid place! All that baroque marble pomposity is an awful aspect of our military past."

Borges was to choose Geneva for his own bones. Exile in Switzerland was preferable to what he perceived as exile in Argentina.

From his mother's room I go into Borges's small cell. It is almost completely dark, except for cracks of light that break through the shutters. I go directly to the window to let some light into the room, and when I open one iron and wood shutter, which apparently has not been moved in years, it comes loose from the window and lands rusty and loud on the floor. In the sudden blaze of light I feel awful, almost frightened like a felon caught in the act. Here I am, tearing apart Borges's bedroom. I manage to set the shutter back on its hinges and find an overhead light. There is nothing in the cell but a cot and the dresser with Susana Bombal's picture.

On the bureau I see the image of a youngish attractive woman, smiling, I presume, for Borges. Here is one, among many, of those handsome literary women whom the poet has attracted around him for much of his life, but who is absent as a subject from his writing. Only in the last years is there, through the presence of María Kodama, a strong nascent romantic element in Borges's poems.

The cot is the literary center of this room, for dream and nightmares, rather than romantic and sensual love, are a central preoccupation in Borges's writing. As I stare at the cot I understand why, whatever is in his mind, the poet will have insomnia and nightmares. Who could sleep through the night on that uneven, sagging mattress atop its flimsy springs? But the inefficient machine for sleep has served Borges well. It contributes to giving him the nether landscape, the world of the ambiguous South in the dream-reality story of the same name, "El sur," or this fine typical poem, "Nightmare," in which he evokes another mirror of himself. Who is the ancient king, from Norway or Northumberland, haunting him even during the day after he has awakened?

> I'm dreaming of an ancient king. His crown
> Is iron and his gaze is dead. There are
> No faces like that now. And ever far
> His firm sword guards him, loyal like his hound.
> I do not know if he is from Norway
> Or Northumberland. But from the north, I know.
> His tight red beard covers his chest. And no,
> His blind gaze doesn't hurl a glance my way.
> From what extinguished mirror, from what ship
> On seas that were his gambling wilderness
> Could this man, gray and grave, venture a trip
> Forcing on me his past and bitterness?
> I know he dreams and judges me, is drawn
> Erect. Day breaks up night. He hasn't gone.

As I stand in the room, I notice the one central object that has eluded my attention, near the picture and over the dresser. The mirror. What is more important for Borges? The mirror, he declares, is a source of copulation and revelation; it gives the one and the other, it distorts and tells the word, it is false and it is infinite. In it everything happens and nothing is remembered, it cannot hold onto time and is deprived of memory, it is always and only now — like external time itself. It is read, like the texts of rabbis, from right to left. It tells who one is. I see the blindman touching the glass for glimmers of himself in "A Blind Man":

> I do not know what face looks back at me
> When I look at the mirrored face, nor know
> What aged man conspires in the glow
> Of the glass, silent and with tired fury.
> Slow in my shadow, with my hand I explore
> My invisible features. A sparkling ray
> Reaches me. Glimmers of your hair are gray
> And some are even gold. I've lost no more
> Than just the useless surfaces of things.
> This consolation is of great import,
> A comfort had by Milton. I resort
> To letters and the rose — my wonderings.
> I think If I could see my face I'd soon
> Know who I am on this rare afternoon.

In this room, among his few essential possessions that regulate his life — the picture dream of youth in the silver frame; the window shuttered against the spring light; the mirror with its x-ray gaze; the cot as a bed of wild dreams, Ryder's "night mare," and Nordic saga — we have some of the ingredients of Borges's intensely intimate life and writing.

Among many readers who know the poet by a few of his best-known stories and essays and a few of the early poems, there is a popular myth that Borges is a cerebral writer, a metaphysician, the decipherer of Pascal's spheres and inventor of memory machines. This portrait of the writer and man is at best a half-truth. The scholar and spoofing pedant and metaphysician of time, of Kabbalistic letters and symbol systems in which the universe is a projection of language, only makes sense if the other Borges is also known, to give resonant meaning to the caricature of the erudite and prankish bibliophile. For just as his name is plural—Borges, not Borge; and it rhymes with nothing but his first name doubled, that is, Jorges—Borges is himself plural. So, along with the mathematician of time and the cerebral master, intensely passionate and despondent, there is the exquisitely calm and wise man who is reconciled to human limitations, and to a godless world that will forever suggest yet disguise its mystery. There is the Borges of Emersonian transcendence, the secular mystic, and (to use his own description of the experience in the sonnet "Spinoza," one of two on his preferred quiet outsider of the mappable heavens) there is the man waiting in the ghetto of his earthly blindness, free from the tyranny of metaphor and myth:

> Here in the twilight the translucent hands
> Of the Jew polishing the crystal glass.
> The dying afternoon is cold with bands
> Of fear. Each day the afternoons all pass
> The same. The hands and space of hyacinth
> Paling in the confines of the ghetto walls
> Barely exists for the quiet man who stalls
> There, dreaming up a brilliant labyrinth.
> Fame doesn't trouble him (that reflection of
> Dreams in the dream of another mirror), nor love,
> The timid love of women. Gone the bars,
> He's free, from metaphor and myth, to sit
> Polishing a stubborn lens: the infinite
> Map of the One who now is all His stars.

Borges is also a child of military men, who dreams of historic Danes invading Scotland and of Norsemen wandering in their blue ships across the coffin seas, and of his own early heroes, including the various Colonel Borgeses who fought and died across the pampas in the complicated wars throughout the nineteenth century.

He is a supporter of military figures and, at the same time, of wistful neighborhood *compraditos* or *guapos* and the knife duelers who inhabit his lowlife stories. Eventually he will abandon these agents of violence—the official ones of the state and the outlaw ones of the barrio. He ceases to write about the lowlife killers and, at the end of his life, disillusioned, he will, we remember, publicly decry his military past, for those ancestors gave Argentina its bloody generals during the Dirty War against the rebels.

And there is the more recognizable Borges of the books, the pen, the library, the man not of the sword but of the cane, who walks with friends in every city of the world, and the public speaker who chats with an audience that wants to hear the old man reveal Borges. There is finally the lonely blindman, cornered in his solitude, unaided by the mirror, his mind too clever to grant him eternity. That figure with dead searching eyes haunts his last five books of poetry, even in the titles *Elogio de la sombra* (In Praise of Shadow) and *Historia de la noche* (History of the Night).

By the time I get back to the dining room where Borges is waiting, it is the hour of the Old English lesson. It is 1975, and Borges has retired from his formal duties at the University of Buenos Aires, where for more than a decade the high school dropout was a professor of Anglo-Saxon language and literature. When Perón came to power and Borges was fired from his modest position as librarian, Borges, then in his fifties and losing his sight, decided to make his living by giving lectures. He also took up Anglo-Saxon, or Old English, as he prefers to call that habit. He began to teach Old English at the university and wrote a book on Germanic literatures, two-thirds of which treats Old English and Scandinavian writings.

He often muses out loud on the interior reasons for learning the tongue of the harsh Saxons, for adding it to his already "weary memory." But there is another reason for learning Old English besides his tremendous sensual love for the language and its elemental narrative verse. His own confined solitude, enriched by more of those unknown words, pushes his soul closer and closer to the immanent universe:

Poem Written in a Copy of Beowulf

At times I ask myself what are the reasons,
During my wandering night, that now impel
Me to begin (expecting no miracle
Of skill) to learn the tongue of the harsh Saxons.
Exhausted by the years my memory
Allows the futilely repeated words
To slip away, the way my life first girds

And then ungirds its weary history.
I tell myself it must be that the soul,
In a sufficient and a secret way,
Knows it is endless, that its vast and grave
Circle takes in and can accomplish all.
Beyond the longing and beyond this verse,
Waiting for me, endless: the universe.

Borges gives his lessons in Old English late on Sunday afternoons. They last about two hours and then he goes out for supper, usually walking off to Adolfo Bioy Casares's place. I have attended the lessons off and on for some five months. The students are regular: an Englishwoman who is an old friend; some former students at the university who now have modest positions in stores or in the local bureaucracy; and María Kodama, who is finishing her doctorate in Old English. The atmosphere is electric.

Borges is seated on the couch under the living room windows. First he chooses some texts from Old English or Old Norse, or (on some more adventurous occasions) from Old Icelandic. Beside him, holding the books with the old texts, is Pablo, who shows him line by line what the group is reading, as if Borges can see and decipher the words. Borges appears to follow, and of course he knows most of the works by heart. Indeed, he has such a facility for memorizing texts that I often wanted to ask him whether he had bothered to read the texts while he was imprinting them in his memory.

After the lesson, he asks what stories from English to read. One or several of us are called upon to read Poe or Hawthorne or James. While Schopenhauer is Borges's Thursday night reading, I remember that his preferred "reading habit" (to use his terminology) involves the authors of the nineteenth-century American renaissance. Unlike any of the major modernists of our century, Borges found his habit, his reading drug, in Melville and Hawthorne, in Emerson and Dickinson, and above all in Whitman. The French and all of Europe, even well into our own time, discovered in America—or invented—only Poe and his "visionary and atrocious wonders."

The atmosphere is, as I said, electric; perhaps that word is an escape from describing the wonderful details of the ambience. Laughter dominates. Borges likes to laugh, but nowhere have I seen him laugh so constantly as when he is enjoying the sounds and meanings of these old northern texts and sharing them with these Old Saxon enthusiasts near the South Pole. Accustomed to working every day, even when traveling, he always finds time for certain pleasures, such as reading Old English with his former students.

"Why did you take up the language of these barbaric crude northerners?" his mother often reproached him. "Why not Greek, the tongue of a civilized people?"

But Borges likes the barbarian. He has little use for the middle class of any country (though "Borges" means a "bourgeois") and seems not to be in the same century with them. He likes the underworld of Buenos Aires and the gaucho and ruffian northern provinces of Argentina and Uruguay. Those lands are more outlaw in his mind than they are in reality, but his early manhood experiences of a trip to the north, of seeing a man shot casually in front of his eyes, his readings from nineteenth-century gaucho poets, Ascasubi and José Hernández's *Martín Fierro*, writers of the pampas, established the stage he was to describe for the next fifty years.

His former student Pablo is now an accountant, and, he tells me, not very high in the banking hierarchy. In America a bank accountant suggests moderate wealth, printouts, authority. Though Argentina is a country of unsinkable natural resources despite bad governments, generals, and wars, a bank accountant there is more often a man or woman who sits behind the tellers, checks on them, studies big graph-paper notebooks, and counts all day. His salary is low. Pablo is attired in something of a poor man's Sunday suit. In a coarse orange sweater, having removed his striped black jacket, he is seated on the couch next to Borges. His round silver glasses frame eyes alert with intelligence and decisive humor. We are speaking half English, half Spanish, and his English is excellent. In a country of classes (though not so rigid as in the rest of Latin America), Pablo is not of the privileged. Although Argentines are great travelers, I am sure he has not left the Republic.

The uncurtained city sky is turning twilight, casting dramatic shadows on the old poet's face. To the left of the couch is the English lady, and to the right, María Kodama, who looks like a lovely creature invented by a brother of Modigliani and Max Beerbohm. Half Japanese, half German, she is Borges's confidant, companion, savior, and future wife. She will undo, on his deathbed, that terrible mistake or infelicitous sin he once committed, which was to marry and marry wrong. María doesn't care to speak much modern English but she is strong in Old English.

First we read the fragment of Finnsburh, the fifty lines that tell the tragic history of Hildeburh, princess of Denmark, whose brother and son die on opposite sides of a treacherous attack. When the Danish warriors fight for five days, their swords glow as if the whole fortress is in flames. Then we read from *The Battle of Maldon* and the Anglo-Saxon bestiary. The panther is Jesus Christ, and his sigh, before he rises to be with his Lord, is a sweet balm. The whale is, as in *Moby-Dick*, Evil and the Devil, and mariners take him to be an island in the sea. When they land on him and light a fire to cook a meal, suddenly the Neighbor of the Ocean, the Horror of the Waters, sinks to the bottom, drowning all the unsuspecting sailors. The whale's proper name is Fastitocalon.

The students do a worthy job deciphering the texts. When there is doubt, they call on the master. But sometimes they have the opportunity to go for information to one of Borges's nineteenth-century Britannicas or to Samuel Johnson's eighteenth-century dictionary — Borges possesses a rare early copy — and these acts of scholarly reference delight all. The commentary is a dessert after the reading.

Occasionally Borges calls on me to read, although he knows I have never studied Old English. Perhaps he is chiding me for having indulged in Greek. (But Borges also loves one ancient Mediterranean language, Latin. He calls it the marble language and claims it is better to have forgotten Latin than never to have studied it at all.) Hardly able to decipher the alphabet, I stumble through the text, aided by Jorge Luis, who clearly enjoys my ignorance. I enjoy it too. Borges is the grandson of a woman from Northumberland and so has a birthright to Old English; it's simply the early speech of his very early ancestors. I have no Saxon or Angle blood, to my knowledge, but this is scarcely an excuse for being the unstudious foreigner.

After Old English we turn daringly to another esoteric pleasure, reading the work of the great Scandinavian writer and coward Snorri Sturluson (1178–1241). Borges likes Snorri Sturluson and his work but especially revels in his name, which he pronounces again and again. He wrote a sonnet about Snorri, who came to understand his cowardice in the darkness of Iceland's salt wind at the instant when the nearby sea (and his hidden assassin) climbed toward his house.

As if to reward me for my amateur efforts at reading the Germanic languages, Borges asks me to read from "The Turn of the Screw." I do so, rather unevenly. The scene comes alive again as I stumble through modern English. María teases me. Pablo reproaches me.

"Don't you have any language, Willis?"

"My mind is elsewhere."

"It's not cookie time yet," chides Isabel, the young woman in stiff gray muslin.

"I have a right to dream," I protest.

"Willis, I pity you," María comforts.

All this attention is going to my head. Suddenly I am saved by a most unusual incident. Although there is abundant targeted assassination in the streets and huge noises almost always mean the guerrilla bombs exploding, there is no security concern in Borges's apartment. Many speculate that the Peronists would like to silence Borges, a gorilla (an opponent of Perón), but fortunately it appears to be out of the question. The scandal of a government off-duty death squad coming around in unmarked Ford Falcons to kill Borges is unthinkable—we hope. But certainly he would be the easiest target, since he walks about the city along the same routes, and of course unguarded. His apartment is open; anyone who knocks at his door comes in. Fanny asks the unknown visitor his or her business and escorts the guest inside.

There is a knock, and a somewhat shabby gentleman enters. We each assume that he is a friend of Borges or of one of us. He talks in a low, conspiratorial voice to Fanny and then heads for the bathroom, where he disappears for some ten minutes. Soon it is clear that no one knows him; but we are confident that eventually he will emerge to reveal the nature of his mission. Time has slowed with anticipation. The gentleman does emerge, at last, but then, with scarcely a look at his living room audience, he grunts goodbye to Fanny and walks out. We giggle at our incomprehension and the absurdity of the coming and going of the unknown toilet user. A little metaphysical play has taken place—and I'm off the reader's hook.

Borges claims that this small episode is proof that he, an elder writer, is becoming a very popular and public man in the republic of Argentina. He further pontificates, "The government, you see, is sending emissaries to evaluate our literary *tertulias.* Why, the word of our workshop has spread like sweet gossip through the nation.

Basic esoteric knowledge of Old English has become important, like hand grenades and maté and holidays. Soon we will be interviewed by live journalists and featured next to the sports heroes in the leading papers. Each one of us is destined to become as famous and familiar to our nation as a tennis player."

"You shock me, Borges," I say. "I didn't know you were such an ambitious nationalist and patriot. I didn't think you believed in nationhood . . ."

"Neither in the *patria* (fatherland) or the *matria* (motherland)," he puns, inventing the word *matria*. "Not in the republic, nor in South America, nor in the universe. These words, well, they are only words. They are superstitions we have come to believe."

We are again descending the circular staircase. I notice that Borges's face, in the half-light, has become, like rain on the uneven pavement, a mirror of distortion. His uneven eyes are filled with this half-light and are childlike as they are grave. As always, I regret saying goodbye. It is a sense of loss I never overcome. We are grouped on the street, all with very friendly but now different personalities, for we are each off to our own society and have already taken on in part the character of the new destination. It is raining a bit. I say goodbye to Borges and María, who begin to walk around the corner to the weekly conversational supper at Bioy Casares's. I head for my flat.

In my rooms I do what I can to preserve my feeling for Borges. In my mind he is now with his invisible beasts. I think of him not at his supper party, but in the flash of his looking up at the ceiling to read an Old Norse word from his memory book. I see him in the yellowish light of the tiger, his preferred color, since in that yellow his dead eyes are often bathed. I also see him in his cell, the insomniac lying on his cot, disdaining death, dreaming of a white deer that has just appeared in a dream poem he wrote a few days ago. He lies quietly, surging from waters to know the panther who cannot die.

A Very Brief
and Fearful Incident

Two French nuns, Alice Doman and Leonie Renée Duquet,
who were giving catechism in the poor barrios, were seized
by the military, tortured at the Escuela de Mecánica Armada,
drugged, and thrown out of a helicopter into the Rio de la
Plata. Later, when democracy was restored under Alfonsín and
the military went on trial, it turned out, as recorded in the
Libro de Juicio (Book of Justice), that "The Little Flying
Nuns" title, which the military had amusingly bestowed on
their victims, came from an American TV serial.

The evenings when I taught American poetry, from Walt
Whitman to James Wright, at the *profesorado* on the Avenida de
Mayo were my joy. Unless it was late, I walked down the big avenues
until I reached the unimposing, rundown building of the *profesorado*,
which my informants swore had the best professors and students of
literature in Argentina. Each floor looked somehow like a basement;
this rich country is not generous about upkeep of its public universities. My students were alert and outgoing, their English excellent,
and one needed no tricks to get them to talk. For the first time I felt
the same dynamic atmosphere as at Columbia, where I remember
one tremendous graduate course on Joyce's *Dubliners* and Dylan
Thomas's late poems. In New York we were all noisy wise guys. Our
numbers included a nun and a rabbi, our classical and biblical experts,
and an encyclopedic group of students who let no allusion or epiphany
go undetected, undocumented, unanalyzed. This was during the sub-
dued '50s, but we were unaware of the silence.

Similarly Buenos Aires, despite the near-war situation, with ex-
plosions occurring so regularly that every slamming door was taken
for a bomb. Despite the horror of the day and the nocturnal murder
squads, the city was alive with crowded bookstores, film houses,
pulsing, noisy streets, with little Isabelita the *presidente* screaming
and mightily amplified as her voice filled the great Plaza de Mayo
and the ears of hundreds of thousands. A huge Egyptian obelisk

overlooked the downtown area, asserting Argentina's right to membership in the club of colonial powers that acquired exotic treasures to enrich their museums, parks, and avenues. The city was also alive with union marches, with workers holding up their fists, smiling macho buddy smiles and enjoying their collective anger. There were excellent concerts, artistic happenings, activities of all kinds, and to all hours. Often, as was my unhealthy habit, I stayed up all night working; when I strayed into the streets at four or five o'clock, there were cafés on every downtown block where I could take a book, read, scribble, and keep going on pastry and blue mugs of coffee.

By contrast, Montevideo and Santiago de Chile, under equally repressive regimes where opposition to the government was comparatively minor, were dead capital cities. Silence was truly palpable. In Santiago, on my way to Easter Island, the midnight curfew caught me in twilight-zone dread until an armored jeep finally stopped. The soldiers leaped out, aimed their automatic weapons at me and my companion, demanded our papers, and broke the silence. In Montevideo, which then had the highest per capita police ratio in the world, or so I read, muted passivity prevailed. When I went for a week to teach four graduate seminars, I had to play games to make the students acknowledge their existence.

One of my favorite students at the *profesorado* was Nelly Shakespeare, an Argentine, part of the large Anglo-Argentine, but very Argentine, community. When the Malvinas war erupted, Borges, himself Anglo-Argentine, said ruefully, "This awful war is a struggle between two old bald men, fighting over a comb."

One evening at the *profesorado* we were reading Dickinson's "I heard a fly buzz when I died." From the courtyard below we heard a mass of students shouting *Perón, Perón, Perón!* The door flew open and two young people rushed in, stood there out of breath, and belligerently commanded us, "Everyone out! Downstairs, in the court! Political rally."

There was a pause. I put Dickinson down.

Nelly calmly got up from her seat and went to the corner door, where the two student officials waited. She said to them, firmly, "This is a graduate seminar. The political rally is only for undergraduates."

"*Ay, dispense.*" "Oh, excuse us," apologized the student leaders, who folded before authority, turned, and ran off to arouse the next class.

That same evening I walked to the other *profesorado* where I was teaching, the Escuela de Lenguas Vivas. Here my class was small, five women, in a pleasant old mansion converted into a college. I was teaching a course in translation theory and practice. After leaving the school, I stopped in a café for a bite. I was tired. I picked up a newspaper, *La Opinión,* and read about the internal war.

The AAA (Alianza Anticomunista Argentina) was working over-time to terrorize. In Rioja a suspect bishop, Enrique Angelelli, had been murdered, as had been Bishop Oscar Romero in El Salvador. Everyone was talking about a Swedish woman, the daughter of a diplomat, who was killed. And more serious for the international reputation of the regime would be the case of Las Monjitas Volantes (The Little Flying Nuns). Two French nuns, Alice Doman and Leonie Renée Duquet, who were giving catechism in the poor barrios, were seized by the military, tortured at the Escuela de Mecánica Armada, drugged, and thrown out of a helicopter into the Rio de la Plata. Later, when democracy was restored under Alfonsín, and the military went on trial, it turned out, as recorded in the *Libro de Juicio* (Book of Justice), that "The Little Flying Nuns" title, which the military had amusingly bestowed on their victims, came from an American TV serial.

Just as I departed through the glass doors of the café, I noticed a commotion in the street. The police, with their high boots of black asparagus and gray uniforms resembling leaves of malignant plants, had blocked off traffic. Other men, plainclothesmen, were standing by their unmarked Ford Falcons. Bent over and facing the stone wall across the street were seven men and women. I was certain they were students. They held their arms overhead, their hands leaned on the wall as they were being searched, kicked, beaten by plainclothes thugs. Some of the uniformed police were joking lightly. Many bystanders watched the drama but could do nothing. It was a didactic advertise-ment of brutality. The oppression, the impotence of the witnesses was overwhelming. I felt destroyed. I knew—we all knew—that these young people would soon disappear for good.

After a few minutes the students were shoved into the waiting Ford Falcons. There wasn't room for one young woman; they dragged her across the gutter from one vehicle to another. Then they pushed her around to the rear of one red Falcon, threw her violently into the trunk, and slammed it. This produced among the assailants an uproar of erotic laughter.

Córdoba Far and Alone

"That picture of him, that late photograph, so pained and, I'd say, honest. Baudelaire suffered. And then he made all those silly, futile gestures to gain respectability at the end. To enter the French Academy. Can you imagine that the champion of Edgar Allan Poe wished to be accepted by the Academy? The photo of Baudelaire, as I remember it, is like another image in all the books, one of Kafka. Do you remember that rather tortured snapshot of Kafka, showing a well-groomed face, but one clearly just coming out of the penal colony?"

In late August 1975 Buenos Aires was coming out of an ugly winter of death squad kidnappings of city dissidents, of guerrilla attacks on naval shipyards and police stations, on army officers in their cars or apartments. In the north, in lush, black magic Jujúi province, and especially in Tucumán, the Trotskyites, ERP (Revolutionary Army of the People), urban *Montoneros,* and student rebels were moving from hit-and-run operations to open field combat. It was not civil war but sporadic operations. It was not yet called the Dirty War, but the Dirty War was already proceeding with implacable cruelty: the night visits and roundups by soldiers or plainclothes police of civilians, their torture and incarceration in "Olympic sports camps" (as the euphemism had it) and their subsequent execution, often by being drugged and dropped from helicopters or planes into the Rio de la Plata or the ocean. Bodies even washed up across the river on the coast of Uruguay.

This was the government of Isabelita Perón. The figure directing police and military operations was López Rega, nicknamed el Brujo (the Warlock) or the Astrologer. López Rega had been Juan Perón's brutal sidekick, and under him he established and headed the dreaded AAA death gangs who toured the streets of Buenos Aires in vehicles with no license plates or other official markings and ripped people out of their houses—especially students, young professionals, artists,

and intellectuals—for immediate miseries and execution. A dispro-
portionate number of those killed were Jews.

With the nation sinking, with prices soaring through black market
inflation, with thousands *disappearing* and other thousands going into
exile to escape death, there was a mood of national depression. Yet,
despite the oppressive facts, to be in Argentina in those days had a
powerful fascination. A country's catastrophes, whether of war, revolution, or any natural or humanly invented violence, ironically create
adventure along with death. I remember my two years in havocked
Greece at the end of its Civil War, a year in repressive early post-
Franco Spain, a month in China during the madness of the "Great
Cultural Revolution." Despite the mayhem and grotesque suffering,
for an observer—and I acknowledge the contagion—it was an essential
experience to be then in these countries in their worst years; and
similarly to be in Argentina, to be with Borges, to share confidences
with friends and participants in the trauma.

Such interest is felt not only by foreign journalists, writers, and
other visitors, but also by many natives who are driven to the fatal
romance of violence. The stupid, horrendous Dirty War was for many
of its participants—on both sides—the crusade, the sacred revolution,
the great adventure. The terrible secret war in Argentina was—like
massive prisons, major earthquakes, the destruction of Tibet during
the Cultural Revolution in China—disguised by the government,
through lies and silence, in massive cover-up. But the concealment
in Argentina, as well as in China, was not only directed by the
government but willingly embraced by a segment of the population
or outside observers. In China the brainwashing tours were enthu-
siastically received by China experts, foreign guests, and friends of
China. (I was a foreign guest there three years before my stay in
Buenos Aires.) In Argentina it was perfectly possible for respectable
burghers, with faith in their military and church, to deny the whispers
of torture and execution. Many, many succumbed to denial. Friends
told me their good Catholic parents could not believe that the essential
institutions of the Argentine nation were conducting the Dirty War.
Even the daily presence of the "Mad Mothers," as they were called,
quietly carrying large photographs of their disppeared children in the
Plaza de Mayo, failed to convince much of the respectable public—
until the very end. These women—largely well dressed and middle
class—who were telling the truth of murder were, for that revelation,

called insane. What epithet should we use for a society or regime that invents the name "Mad Mothers" to disguise official homocide?

One very important factor contributing to the implausible denial of mass violence was the appearance of safety and security in the capital city. Despite the nightly thud of exploding bombs in Buenos Aires, order in the capital was not an illusion of carefully placed mirrors. The city remained, except for those specifically targeted for assassination or kidnapping, one of the safe large cities in the world to walk in, at any time of day or night.

Platenses (natives of the Rio de la Plata River basin) like to stroll their City of Good Winds. Buenos Aires's streets are always crowded. It is nothing like a sleek, tall downtown commercial Houston, hermetically empty and fearful after dark. I would stroll the streets of the capital and its outlying neighborhoods at midnight or at three in the morning with no apprehension of danger. And Buenos Aires remained a vibrant, sophisticated city of publishers, concerts, periodicals, bookstores (though Freud as well as Marx were banned on bookshelves and in university psychology and political science courses); a city of interesting old neighborhoods, the elegant traffic-free main commerical street of La Calle Florida, superb restaurants in abundance, noodle stores, theater, maté. There was the tango presiding on the radio, the *lunfardo* spoken in the streets; the Rio de la Plata inlets for waterskiing, or weekends in primitive vacation huts along the great river. There were the intellectuals, the mania for cultural gatherings and happenings, the dinners, the Semana del Fracaso (the Week Honoring Failure), the writer and journalist friends. And finally there was Borges.

For a Spanish-speaking outsider, Argentina was, I confess, also my adventure. As in my last year in China, I counted with regret the days before the morning that would mark my departure. In August 1975 I went as a Fulbright lecturer to two universities in Buenos Aires. Friends had warned me not to go. Or take a bulletproof vest. Wrong advice. During my first weeks I did feel an unanticipated disappointment. Mexico I knew through my Mexican stepfamily and student years there; Inca Peru I knew through earlier trips. After Mexico and Peru, with their vast pre-Columbian culture, Argentina initially seemed devoid of that extraordinary Indian antiquity, and consequently poor in mystery.

Soon I discovered the old colonial cities, particularly Córdoba. Like

Quito, Lima, Mexico City, the cities of Argentina begin their post-conquest life in the sixteenth century, but without the temples of Yucatán, Tical, or Machu Picchu. Through *Martín Fierro,* the gaucho writers, and Borges, however, I learned about other Argentinas. The wasteland *páramos* of Patagonia and the Argentine/Brazilian and Argentine/Uruguayan rich wildernesses in the north should fill the imagination of the dullest outsider. And there was Buenos Aires.

When I reached my downtown hotel, the phone rang. The sister and companion of an Argentine student friend of mine back in Indiana were waiting downstairs.

"Come up."

"The hotel will not permit two women to come up to a man's room."

"I'll be right down."

María Elena and Isabel were my first friends in Buenos Aires. They took me to a restaurant where the tables were butcher blocks and the Argentine-cut steaks were served not on plates but on the wooden stumps. Although I eat little red meat, steak in Argentina is the best temptation for that unhealthy vice. The poorest brawny industrial worker, whom one might see tramping in military defiance in a labor protest march down Santa Fe, would think himself starving—as a Pole without sausage—if supper didn't include steak.

"Pretty strict country about sexual freedom," I commented.

"We are very proper," smiled Isabel, who with María Elena owned a small foreign language lab on Corrientes for learning English.

"There is still a generational silence between children and parents," María Elena added, "between us and our Italian immigrant or Argentine Spanish elders. They profess Catholic values of chastity and abstinence, but no one practices those virtues, other than the maimed and the impotent. We are the freest, most easygoing of Latin American countries about these things. Yet we argue with our respectable padres about sex, and there are these quaint hotel rules. It's all fake. A veneer in a wild and open society which has, consequently, less prostitution and illegitimacy than our neighboring 'chaste' societies in Latin America. We're as sexually liberated as Sweden, but most of our elders won't admit it."

"María Elena, you're a textbook."

"No, just a language lab."

Argentines, I discovered, unlike most North Americans, have a passion for defining their nation and their people, whose character is always changing.

My first rented room in Buenos Aires got me into a hilarious predicament. It was the apartment of a middle-class, rather educated lady who lived with her twenty-year-old son. I had to be in by a certain time, because they could provide me with no extra key to the outside entrance. In the apartment I could not read or write for more than short periods, because my *dueña* wanted to teach me new tango steps or talk about Perón or how Argentines were really Europeans and not Indians like people in the rest of South America or, worse, blacks. Soon she became amorous; I was blind to her good intentions. The *dueña* was furious with me, but I made my escape to another apartment, now all my own, cheerful, with good light, cheap because of the inflating currency. It was on Paraguay, about three minutes up the street from Borges's place on Maipú.

The *portero* (concierge-doorman) at the new apartment house amazed me. I had lived in many countries of Spanish America, three years in Spain, and felt comfortable in Castillian. I lectured in Spanish at my university. I also feel comfortable with the quickest Andalusian or Caribbean Spanish, when half the consonants are swallowed for dessert. But when I first spoke to the *portero,* his *lunfardo,* or city dialect, threw me. I was downcast. I rushed upstairs and turned on the radio to make sure I had not suffered language aphasia. Then I called Isabel to receive linguistic consolation. I'd get used to it, she said. And I did.

Moreover, I loved the slang, especially the taxi drivers' mastery of invective. Each stoplight and bus squeezing us over while pumping fumes from its side muffler into our open cab would bring genius to the driver's tongue. *¡Pucha madre!* (Whore mother!) or *¡boludo!* and *pelotudo!* (two almost identical ways of saying "big-balled idiot") were the commonest flatteries.

Even though politics was murderous, it was also a source of black humor, and I heard a hundred jokes about deputies, ministers, Isabelita, generals. I kept up by reading the papers. After making myself a quick breakfast, my early morning pleasure was to buy several papers and read them with urgency. I read the liberal, literary, courageous *La Opinión* (in quality and appearance like *Le Monde* of Paris or *El*

País of Madrid), which still came out daily despite the murders of several of its journalists. *La Opinión* was published by Jacobo Timerman, who was later imprisoned and tortured, but saved from execution through Jimmy Carter's personal intervention. Timerman wrote his eloquent, elemental, and terrifying book—*Man without a Name, Cell without a Number*—about his incarceration.

I also kept up with the life of the nation through journalist friends. Mort Rosenblum, then head of United Press International for Argentina, Chile, and Uruguay, was my closest American friend. From Mort I got everything. Even the last breaths of Franco came over his wires one morning just as I phoned. Mort's editorial office had huge posters of Perón and Isabelita on the walls—a protection just in case. He had a German shepherd, Zeke, whom he had acquired a few years earlier with UPI in Zaire. Zeke could, on command, open a complicated front door and usher a guest into his apartment on Avenida Libertador. Some days before Christmas, Mort returned from Montevideo, where he had interviewed the Uruguayan Minister of Security, the official in charge of police and Uruguayan murder squads. After supper he treated us to a record of American Big Band sounds that was a gift from the Minister. The disk contained "Los Hits de Glenn Miller," played horrendously by the National Police Band of Uruguay.

That same evening I saw Jimmy Pringle, the *Newsweek* bureau chief, who came with Juan de Onís, the *Times* man. Pringle had been my friend and guide in Beijing in 1972 when he was with Reuters. In 1984–85, we were again both living and working in China. Jimmy treated me one summer night in 1985 to the best meal I have had in Asia. He had arranged to take me the next day to Prince Sihanouk, whom I admired for many reasons, but I couldn't put off a two-month trip to the Chinese Turkestan and Tibet for which the arrangements had been so difficult and so delicate. In Buenos Aires as in Asia, Pringle knew politicians and revolutionaries, from the Dalai Lama and Madam Mao to leaders of the Khmer Rouge whom he interviewed deep in the Cambodian jungle during a meal for which runners had brought in ice to keep the bottled drinks tasty and the interviewer impressed.

Of course, most of my friends were Argentine. The novelist and poet Mario Satz was my most intimate companion. After teaching my two-hour evening course on American poetry at the dumpy but exciting *profesorado* on Avenida de Mayo, I would race off in a cab to an auditorium where Mario was giving a course on the Kabbalah. Often I'd fall asleep as soon as I sat down on the hard wood seat. There'd been no time to grab a bite to eat on route. I was exhausted, embarrassed about dozing off, and inspired when I could keep awake. By the second hour of Mario's lecture I was awake and alert. Afterward we'd go out to eat in one of the endlessly good "ordinary" restaurants of Buenos Aires, where we would talk poetry, publishers, Kabbalah, women, and astrology, which he knew historically in its many religious origins.

Mario was handsome, mesmerizing, a polymath of esoterica and languages. He took me everywhere: to lectures, to concerts, to rather ostentatious lawn parties where I chatted mainly with rebels and writers. Doubleday was about to publish his novel *Sun* in English translation. In some gatherings people told me dangerously compromising facts of their lives, their politics and secret activities. Here, I was glad I was immediately recognized, accepted; it was flattering. Yet it was strange that in an ambience where informers mingled even among artists and students, and disclosure could mean death, how, at a party, it was perfectly clear to my hosts and others that I, a stranger, could be trusted. In the desperate atmosphere one had to make choices to survive; life would otherwise have been intolerable. The corpses of the young on the cold stone, those tortured corpses that relatives were often brought to witness as a phase of the tactics of terror, also attest to the penalty of inevitable errors in judgment about who was or was not an informer.

Mario had often heard Borges give public lectures but had not spoken to him personally. We went one Sunday morning to Borges's apartment, and the two of them were like children exchanging the secrets of the esoteric Kabbalah. Bells rang in Borges's rooms that morning, as if Isaac Luria of Spain had just then opened spiritual shop in Safed; as if Maimonides in the *judería* of Córdoba were revealing to us, through a spare copy of his *Guide of the Perplexed*, how God was pure intellect; as if the poet Judah Halevi of Tudela were among us, telling how he longed to go to the Holy Land of spikenard and apple peace, of wonder and its courage, and to know his heart in prison was at last flying in a sweet wind into the East.

Borges was the center of the Argentine experience.

There was never a phone call from Borges that did not key me up. The ride on the slow elevator to the sixth floor was an eternity of anticipation. Where would our talk lead us? In the Kabbalist tradition, God created words first in order to do the other deeds. Talking with Borges was a throw of the dice in which the roll might not result in the usual 2 to 12, but 1 or 0, or 00, or 13.

And there were also the ordinary things to be done. I was glad when I could be of some use — writing letters or phoning the States about trips and lectures. He asked me to go with him to his lectures in Buenos Aires, to dinners, on Sunday morning walks to bookstores, Christmas suppers, Old English classes, evening strolls, to share late coffee in the Saint James Café when most places were closed. To accompany him for a few days to the city of Córdoba.

I also cannot deny the anxiety that went along with the exhilaration. I observed how some of Borges's close friends — di Giovanni, Donald Yates, Ricardo Barnatán, Carlos Cortínez — after a while fell away. Borges resented their help, their devotion, and was even enraged by what he perceived to be his entrapment in their care. By the nature of our intimate raillery, his grave and light observations that he shared with me as secrets, by our camaraderie in Argentina and on other continents, our ceaseless talk about language and literature, by his sadnesses — especially in the last years — that he revealed naturally, I felt *confianza,* which in Spanish and French (*confiance*) means a quality of full trust. I don't recall a moment of silence that settled on us, even as respite. Yet there were worries, insecurities, sometimes deeper than I wished. I tried to leave them behind, attributing them to unworthy weakness and neurosis. There was the history of fallen friends.

Most curious among his foreign friends is the separation of one who was never "fallen," who always remained in the center of Borges's most desired virtue and emotion, friendship. Yet Anthony Kerrigan knew Borges only at the beginning and end of his literary career. Kerrigan introduced Borges to the English-speaking world through *Ficciones* and then *A Personal Anthology,* subsequently translating four more books, including his very last volume, *Atlas.* Their acquaintance almost fell away before it took place. There was a brief meeting in Madrid. Thereafter they had a friendship for thirty-two years in absentia, sustained by letters, publications, and unusual messengers. They had near encounters. Tony even wrote an article about *not* meeting Borges in Madrid, and about how on several occasions

Borges embraced the bearer of his greetings effusively, thinking that messenger to be the Kerrigan he was not meeting in person.

Mark Mirsky, the editor of *Fiction,* has told of having supper at an expensive restaurant in New York with Max Frisch, the Swiss novelist, and Borges, as well as others whom Mirsky describes as "the literary brokers of New York." The latter were smugly disparaging Anthony Kerrigan's translations. Mirsky was furious at the pettiness, at their bad judgment, and records the scene in a memoir:

> Tony has still not met the writer he had translated and admired. I could not resist a sudden lunge at Borges, with whom I felt I had made no contact at all. "I want to extend," I called as loud as I could through the tinkling silverware and scraping of chairs, as if the Argentine were half deaf, not blind, "Greetings from Tony Kerrigan."
>
> "Tony?" whispered Borges incredulous.
>
> "Tony Kerrigan," I shouted.
>
> "Tony Kerrigan," cried Jorge Luis Borges across from me and fell halfway over the table to grasp me in his arms, throw them around my neck, kiss my cheeks. "Tony! My benefactor! Tony, my benefactor!"
>
> It was a minute or so before I was able to explain that I was only bringing him greetings from Tony Kerrigan instead of standing there as Anthony in the flesh. The faces at the end of the table were redder than the wine." (Kerrigan, "Autobiography," 212)

In 1980 I gave the introduction to a talk between Borges and interlocutors at the New York PEN Club. After the conversation I saw Tony milling around in the adjoining room. I asked him whether he'd spoken to Borges. Glumly he said that the rivalry, the jealousy of Borges's protectors (in this instance, the other speakers) had turned him off. I couldn't get him into the next room, though in retrospect, given the felicity and dramatic importance of their constant meetings before Borges's death, I should have seized his elegant sleeve and dragged him discreetly into the hubbub around Borges, and given him a push. Yet once more, in New York, he missed Borges.

With all those unseen encounters in printed pages and letters, I thought Kerrigan should be the essential friend, and to be deprived of that intellectual companionship would be a loss for Borges. As it turned out, Borges and Kerrigan finally got together by chance; both were invited to a conference on Freud in Milan. It was the last critical year in Borges's life. They were also together in Rome. Tony, Borges's first and last translator, was also his last close friend in the months before his death.

Most of the time Borges was with his work, his friends; his solitude, which contained all his Spinoza galaxies and Schopenhauer despair; his metaphysical algebras, loneliness, and extinctions. But sometimes there were the normal episodes in everyday life that bothered him immensely, particularly anything that had to do with Perón or Peronismo or with someone he felt might be cheating him because of his blindness or dependence. When I saw Borges's rare but quite sudden angers, I and those who might have been with him tried to be helpful and persuasive, of course to no avail. I remember how, in late November, Borges thought he had been duped at Maxim's. He certainly was not, but he couldn't be convinced otherwise. The owner and the waiter who had served him for a decade came to the apartment, swearing a misunderstanding, offering that he could happily eat there free on a permanent basis. But Borges would not eat there after the "incident" occurred.

In Buenos Aires I felt immensely at home, yet sometimes, I confess, immature and childlike in my enthusiasm for Borges. The normal feeling of pleasure in being with him overcame the inevitable distracting and worthlessly negative emotions.

I liked to work with him late at night on his projects. When we finished, I would read him Kipling or Henry James or Wallace Stevens and some of my Greek and Chinese poets. He would be wearing his open-collared white dress shirt. I don't remember seeing him in anything like casual clothes; his notion of informality, at least with friends, was to remove his suit jacket. He knew where all the books were located on his shelves and would ask me to bring one or the other, and sometimes a phone number he might have had someone write on the inside back cover of Thoreau or Swinburne. He claimed that after nearly thirty years of blindness he could no longer write, though sometimes he scrawled something in the flyleaf of a book. I never asked him for an inscription, but once María gave me a book with a good message. She wrote it, and he signed what I called his Chinese seal character.

One night we were sitting at the dining room table. We had worked late, and Borges was in a mischievous mood when he said, "Do you understand the song of birds?"

"I'm not Saint Francis," I said. "You mean the beauty of the melody?"

"No. The words, the language. They must be saying something. Do you think they are doing all that crooning for nothing?"

"Do you understand the cry of the nightingale?" I countered.

"With my feeling for music," he said, "I'm more likely to be hearing crows."

"I knew a crow in Zurich whose name was George," I said, "and he talked all the time like a parrot. Better than a parrot. We conversed in a very lively way. George was mainly interested in worms and the weather. Maybe George was your Swiss double?"

"But I haven't been discovered talking with crows," Borges protested. "Not that I remember. Nor have I even dreamt of conversing with crows. I'm old fashioned, you know. Yet if you upgraded George to a raven, I could possibly imagine a raven as my Swiss double."

"Nevermore!"

"Poor Poe. I owe so much to him. We all do. After all, he invented the detective novel. But listen here," he said. "If you can't understand birds when they sing, if you can't even understand birds, mind you, have you ever thought what they think of us when they hear us talking? I'd say there's a profound misunderstanding between birds and humans. We must sound absurd to them!"

"It's true. If I were a bird, I'd be disappointed with human voices. Especially yours, Borges. I'm positive the birds must gossip about your throaty baritone, saying Who's that walking foghorn? He sounds worse than an old gutter frog."

"Barnstone, you seem to have an inside track. I'd say you were hanging out with the fighting cocks in Palermo."

"Borges, you unduly honor me, but you're foolish. Imagine me with the great fighting cocks of your Palermo. More accurately I should say you're a silly old blindman. A little bird told me so."

I felt embarrassed about my platitude, but Borges liked trite phrases just as he relished "improper" Spanish, from *milonga* to *lunfardo*. I remembered what Lorca said about music—that he was crazy about bad music and wondered whether one day he'd also be crazy about bad poetry.

"Have I offended you?" I asked.

"Oh, very much so. I am smarting. But I like being called silly. Who would have thought so? Somehow on this evening it gives me hope."

Alicia Jurado, the novelist, biographer of W. H. Hudson, president of the Argentine PEN, and very long-time friend of Borges, with whom she collaborated to write a book on the Buddha, called me. Would I like to accompany her and Borges to Córdoba? Borges had been invited to give a lecture on the theme of time. The trip and lecture were arranged by Señor Olocco, who also arranged for a book signing sale afterward at his own bookstore. Alicia had the handsome face of Jawaharlal Nehru. Even something in her hairdo made her look East Indian like her hero Siddhartha. Borges said her nose was straight as that of the Jack of Spades, and maybe classically Greek. So much for Alicia's nose and hair.

I liked Alicia. She was aristocratic, tough, but eager to be led away from her formality. We often ate together, and later she came to America and stayed for a week in our barn. I did a photographic portrait of her and Borges, which she used in a critical volume on the poet. Alicia was on the far right politically. Even Borges, who gave himself no political epithet, said she was conservative. She was a bad source of information for him during the Dirty War. I argued with her that PEN—and she was its president—should be screaming about the "disappeared" writers, but PEN in Argentina never spoke out, failing in a desperately crucial mission and duty. In other countries—Poland and South Korea, for example—PEN carried out vigorous campaigns to publicize and seek the release of writers in prison, regardless of potential government retribution against PEN.

Our plane was to leave for Córdoba at 8:15 in the morning. Borges was packed and ready when I reached his apartment at 6:45. Alicia, a good traveling companion, came a few minutes later. She looked tall and happy. In the fellowship of dawn, we all felt adventure, including Fanny, who was combing Borges's hair.

Borges was in very good spirits despite a night of little sleep. "I wasn't wakened by my usual nightmare, but by a bomb, a few buildings away. It happened about 2:30 in the morning, and very loud. I couldn't get back to sleep, so I conceived the plot of a short

story. I had to do it in my head. The beginning and end—they come in a flash; later I fill in the middle."

"What was the story?"

"As I was working it out, I must have slipped back into a dream, but it didn't seem to matter. This very curious incident took place. I was tramping through downtown London, looking for a bed-and-breakfast place. I had only a few days to work in the British Library, and not much money. Above a chemist's shop I found a shabbily respectable place and quickly arranged for my room, encouraged to do so by the owner, who invited me to afternoon tea, which I readily accepted. When this tall, ugly, intense man had me alone, he said, 'I have been looking for you.' What he had up his sleeve I couldn't tell, but his glare almost paralyzed me. In those days, at least in the hour of my dream, I could see perfectly well.

" 'What do you want from me?'

" 'Just a thousand pounds.'

" 'You can't get what I don't have. If I had it, I wouldn't be in your rundown quarters,' I said to him defiantly.

" 'I'm not here to steal. I'm here to make you the happiest man in the world, and only because you are worthy of it.'

" 'Giving you a sack of money won't make me happy,' I informed him.

" 'I have just acquired Shakespeare's memory.'

" 'It was as if the tiger came out of the closet. I had no idea what he meant.

" 'If you are willing to forget who sold it to you, or that you ever laid eyes on me or stayed in my rooms, I will go ahead with the transaction.' "

"What happened?" I asked.

"I took his bundle of papers, read one gloriously lucent page, picked up the phone and wired Buenos Aires for my savings, cleaning out my miserly lifetime account. By then I could not remember a word of the burning text of Shakespeare's memory, and the multiple shocks woke me up. Unlike my nightmares, when I'm obliged to wait them out even when recognizing myself in an old scene, this time I came out of my Shakespeare business quick, clean, and empty handed. Except for the story."

Between the times of my coming and our going, the elevator broke down.

"Then we walk," Borges announced, and so we descended the six flights in the dark, Borges tapping ahead cheerfully with his cane. I was amazed at how his story had invigorated him. He gripped the rail, dragging us with him, Alicia hanging onto me. When we hit daylight again, we hailed a cab and were off to the domestic airport.

For all our efficient rush, once at the counter we were told that the plane would leave at 9:15, an hour late. Borges didn't care. As we stood chatting, he was anxious to convince me that the Córdobans were very good people, with *gracia,* with the best sense of humor in Argentina, and that the city was *linda.*

The bus for the plane came. The poet was used to climbing steep stairs, and with the help of passengers pushing him gently up, we found ourselves on board. The motor started, roaring away. We stood for about thirty minutes, crammed in the stiffling but immobile bus. Borges said it was a long trip; he was surprised to find ourselves in the same spot. Finally the driver got out and disappeared. After another quarter-hour we were asked to descend from the sardine can. A half-hour later we were asked to board again; this time we circled the whole airport to reach the *confitería* (a snack shop) only thirty meters from where we had started. The morning held its enigmas.

Engine trouble had necessitated the trip to the snack shop. And the mechanics were on strike. The day before, the city was festooned with confetti and marching workers from the SMATA syndicate, who were protesting the larger metallurgical union that was attempting to take it over and that had just tried to assassinate its leader. Now no one knew whether our delay was caused by engine trouble, the strike, or national politics.

The flight was announced for 9:45, 10:30, 11:30, 12:15, 3:00. We waited at a table, eating ham-and-cheese sandwiches, drinking *café con leche,* and talking endlessly. What could be better?

We discussed time, the subject of his lecture. And perfection. He was intimate one moment, joking the next, then grave. He was childlike, excited, maturely wise, stubborn, gentle, wistful. His mood changed like his face. When he spoke of his preferences — Heraclitus, Chesterton, Sophocles, Milton — his taste and modernity were periodless. As we settled down I pulled out an anthology of English poetry and read him Wordsworth, and then Frost's "Neither Far Out Nor In Deep." He repeated lines he liked, his voice filling the words with sonorous importance. He loved Donne's phrase "O my America," which he called "prophetic verse."

"By the way, my eyes are improving," he said.

As a result of a series of injections, Borges believed he was seeing slightly better.

"I make out your nose. It's pointed, no? And there is your eye and your chin," he said, touching my face. "And what's that? Barnstone, are you wearing a tie?"

"Yes, I am."

"How about swapping?"

Alicia was alarmed. She considered my wool tie too wintry in weight and too summery in color for Borges.

"Of course, I'll swap. But are you serious?"

"Borges serious? Some people say I am an ethical man. Is that being serious?" He was almost singing. "I think I am not a serious man."

"It's true, you're rather lightweight—but a friendly literary buff."

"I was worried for a moment," he blurted out. "I wouldn't want to be known as serious. Not serious, mind you!"

I took off my tie and gave it to him. He removed his. Since his mother had died, he'd been wearing only black ties. This one was faded, thin, a misery of a tie, a present from an Anglo-Argentine writer friend, William Shand. Not his most elegant attire. Often Borges dressed like a formal Andalusian lord. On his American trips his suits were sober but in warmer colors, and of fine wool, and his ties, red or blue, were chosen by María. He put on my beige wool tie, one I was fond of.

"I think I am wearing a mattress around my neck. If we stay here any longer I'll stretch out on it. What do you say?" he asked.

"I'll get you a pillow."

Normally, Borges took a nap in the afternoon. After the first seven hours of waiting, he was weary. Alicia Jurado was at first indignant, then furious, finally weary herself. She began to write a letter of complaint to the editor of the newspaper *La Prensa.*

"*Why,* Alicia, when there are so many things wrong with our country?"

Alicia responded by saying that all Peronists are gangsters and should be killed, along with the *montonero* guerrillas, the People's Revolutionary Army, and the rest of the half-hearted politicians. "And the rapists too," she added.

"But who would be left?" Borges asked.

For about an hour Borges sat by himself in the dinky, dreary airport cafeteria. He was as much alone as in his apartment. As I record this, I am looking at a photograph of Borges in the cafeteria. Behind him the black chairs out of focus look like a surrealist piano. The white cuff of his left sleeve almost touches his cane. He is resting both hands on the cane, in a characteristic waiting position. His shirt collar gleams above his suit coat. He is looking straight ahead. From this angle, only his dead left eye is visible. He is looking out the way a tiger waits, thoughtful, unrevealing, accustomed to infinity.

As Borges sat impassively I knew he was not inventing a story or poem. Or was he? Perhaps he had just bought Shakepeare's soul, discovered along with an old unknown edition of Thomas Traherne's *Centuries of Meditations* at the bottom of a London bookbarrow. But as I watched him, with those eyes looking out and seeing only the yellowish blur, I began to remember "The God's Script," one of his tales in which there is a bliss of understanding. The speaker is a Mayan, Tzinacán, from the time of the conquistador Pedro de Alvarado, who has devastated the country and put Tzinacán in a prison made of stones. So many years have passed that he has no way of counting time. He is the last priest of piety, who has used his obsidian knife on the chests of his victims. But that was long ago—though not so long ago as the first day of creation, which he can now imagine. The years of darkness have made him a poet or a visionary, for he has seen God in a blazing light, in a sword or in the petal circles of a rose. In a single felicitous moment he understands the script of the tiger. Ecstasy does not repeat its symbols; the days will obliterate him, and no other life will understand the formula. Nevertheless, he has understood.

Borges has been dreaming this story. No, it was dreamt thirty years earlier, but he is still trying to steal the information from Tzinacán the Indian priest. He has even forgotten the name he gave his imprisoned hero. (He doesn't reread his stories; that is for others to do.) The poet is erect and lost in respectability while concocting his plan to retrieve information from an old fable, from a savage priest whom he has let linger in that cell. In the airport cafeteria that ravaged Indian, tortured by the civilized Alvarado, the handsome one of the portraits can, for twenty minutes, allow him a timeless gaze, a glimpse through the bliss of understanding.

"I hate to wake you from reverie, Borges, but we are leaving."

"How will I give the lecture? It's already five o'clock. This fellow Olocco is rich and, by the way, a scrooge."

Alicia, Borges, and I boarded the plane. It was six in the evening before we reached Córdoba, and at the airport was Olocco. I couldn't help being pedantically amused by his Italian name, which to me phonetically meant "The Madman" by a combination of Greek "O" for "the" and Spanish "loco" for "mad." Olocco put on thick glasses and hurried off with us. He, too, had spent all day at an airport.

We roared through the attractive old colonial city, passing an equestrian statue with its conquistador, Cabrera y Carabajal, founder of the city and Borges's ancestor. Something about Olocco was wrong; I was suspicious. We drove toward the theater where Borges was to give his *charla* (talk). Despite the all-day delay, it was packed. The crowd, by instinct and too much experience, also knew something was wrong. A week earlier the AAA had dragged nine students out of their dormitory, bound them, shot them, and dumped their bodies outside the city. The students were supposed to have been leftists, but the thugs had seized the wrong victims. These were all foreign students from Peru and other Spanish American countries. It was a scandal, even in Perón's Argentina.

As we came near, our vehicle slowed. Two or three hundred young people who had been unable to jam into the theater spotted us. They began to stamp their feet in the street, cheering, shouting, *Borges! Borges! Borges!*

We should have stopped right then. Olocco stepped on the gas and we sped on. I was furious. Borges kept saying, "I have never heard people shouting *Borges* in the street." He was astonished, pleased with the shouting, and confused about where we were going. "What about my *charla?*" he said to me.

"Turn around," I told Olocco. "Let's go back to the theater."

"We must go on to the bookstore," Olocco said. "There's no time for the lecture, I'm sorry to tell you. I have a store full of clients who have been waiting all afternoon for Borges."

"Turn around!"

I would have grabbed the wheel, but I was sitting in back with Borges. Olocco was betraying Borges and the people in the theater.

"The problem is security. There are too many people inside that theater, and also there're all those hooligans in the streets. Most of them students. The auditorium seats only 500; already 700 people are jammed inside. You can be sure the authorities won't allow the lecture."

"*Mentiras*—You're lying," I said to him.

We kept going.

"Look here, Barnstone, I don't like this," Borges told me in English. "This is serious. I came here to speak, not to sign books."

"He's a miser, all right, You were perfectly right about him."

"*No me gusta,*" Borges repeated. "*No me gusta nada.* These people have been waiting for me to talk today. Of course, I would probably give them a very poor talk, but that would not sway them. They have gone in there prepared to appreciate anything I say, and while they would be wrong about me, I couldn't change their pleasant reception. People are very generous with me."

"Because of this scoundrel, today they won't have a chance to be generous."

"I was nervous, but I had it all in my head. I was going to speak about time."

"Not this time, Borges. This *boludo* is a dog."

"Barnstone, you are very harsh on dogs."

At Olocco's store the poet dutifully signed seventy or eighty complete works. This first edition of his complete works was as expensive as it was ugly, but it was useful to have. The frontispiece showed a terrible picture of Borges, a prisoner shot in a dark jail, who couldn't shave or smile. As always, the poet behaved with smiling dignity as each person handed him a book to autograph. It was rare when he didn't exchange a few words with each unseen face.

"Let's go," Borges said to Alicia and me as soon as there was a break in the signing. He insisted on getting our own taxi and we left for our hotel.

Borges was immensely bored, distracted, though dignified. As we waited and waited in the hotel lobby, he looked not old but profoundly tired and sunken into himself. I had not seen him like that before. We entered the dining room, sat down, and some of his old friends showed up. Somehow he recovered his strength in their company, and even before we had anything to eat he was talking, joking, laughing, exchanging stories. Then at the supper table several people again lent him eyeglasses, which he tried on one after another. He was clowning and joyful. His doctor had told him not to play games with his eyes, for fear of straining them. But for the moment he thought he could see better with these chance glasses. I handed him my gold wire-rims. He said they improved his vision. I was skeptical, but he wore them for the rest of the evening. That night, despite madman Olocco's trickery, Borges was enormously playful.

"How did you sleep?" I asked Borges in the morning.

"I slept well for the first time in two months."

I had given him some pills and suggested he take half of one.

"Normally I have two nightmares. But when I have a nightmare, at least I know I have slept a little, and I say to myself in the nightmare, 'Look, now I am not suffering from insomnia.' Either I am in a street and crowds are crushing me or I'm in a house and moving from one room into another, endlessly. The first nightmare is more frightening."

We sat in the dining room, alone. We were having a hilarious breakfast, conspiring against the world. Borges derided the talk he never gave, his timeless speech.

"Borges, you tell me that, without notes, you worry about forgetting the main point when you give a lecture. Last night you achieved perfection: you forgot nothing."

"And remembered nothing. But, look here, there's something even more remarkable: I also said nothing untrue. My silence had the beauty of invisible poetry. Invisible like illusion, which you must understand is the basis of what we dream as reality."

Borges was mocking the world, beginning with himself. He talked about a fashionable nineteenth-century Argentine poet, now forgotten.

"*El pobre. Lo unico que le quedaba era la perfección*" — "Poor man. The only thing he had left going for him was perfection," Borges said, devastatingly.

"And you, Borges, what do you have left?"

"Not perfection," he said. "That is certain. Was Whitman perfect? How boring to be perfect! Whitman was wrong in his verse, as even Frost was wrong, often wrong. They could afford to be wrong, and took the chance. That is why they are such good poets. You know, Willis, your Baudelaire whom you like so much. *He* was always perfect; at least his rhymes were. So even in his best poems we have again and again *coeur, langueur, tenebres, funebres,* and all the expected clichés."

While Borges was deriding the very notion of perfection I remembered Tzvetan Todorov's praise of imperfection in science. Even the notion of absolute truth contradicts science's reason for being; imperfection is a guarantee of survival. To me, imperfection is equally important in art, a necessity for a live poem.

"Come on, Borges. You're right to attack perfection, but so unfair to Baudelaire, who had more guts, more originality than anyone of his day. He could afford some trite rhymes. You yourself are proud of using 'simple' rhymes. Why do you allow Whitman his mistakes but burn Baudelaire for a few clichés? And toward the end, you know, after he stopped dreaming of islands and happiness, there are his extraordinary poems of the poor, the sick, the hopeless inhabitants of the city..."

"But you know I admire Charles Baudelaire," he interrupted. "How could I not? But you must allow me my eccentricity too. Don't I have an English grandmother? That picture of him, that late photograph, so pained and, I'd say, honest. Baudelaire suffered. And then he made all those silly, futile gestures to gain respectability at the end. To enter the French Academy. Can you imagine that the champion of Edgar Allan Poe wished to be accepted by the Academy? The photo of Baudelaire, as I remember it, is like another image in all the books, one of Kafka. Do you remember that rather tortured snapshot of Kafka, showing a well-groomed face but one clearly just coming out of the penal colony?"

"Hola."

It was Olocco. The wretched bookseller was insisting on paying Borges for his nonlecture. He offered the equivalent of $15. It was unimaginable. Borges would have none of it.

"No, no, no!" Borges argued with him.

Borges didn't care to be cheated, and I wondered how he would handle this small matter. He was in splendid shape this morning.

"Olocco, are there any charities in this city?"

"Yes," the bookseller replied, pompously. "Why, we have charities for cancer, leprosy, and the blind."

Borges's face glowed. He told me in English that he was not going to let this man force money on him for his lecture of silence.

"Tell me now, Alicia, are you leprous?"

"Borges!" Alicia exclaimed.

"Alicia, are you presently cancerous?"

"No!" she said with bemused fascination. "What are you up to?" she challenged him, doggedly. Alicia was very pointed when she wished to be. One didn't ignore her with impunity. But, turning his back to her, Borges looked directly at Olocco, staring him down.

"Señor Olocco. La señora Jurado tells me that she is not leprous. She also tells me that she is not cancerous. I am very gratified to hear these affirmations of good news, as I am sure you must be. Now, since I have asked about possible donations to charities beyond my own experience, I must now think selfishly. Give the money to the blind."

At that he got up, wished the gentleman goodbye, and we all went outside. There waiting for us was Borges's friend Carlos Alvarez, the lawyer who had handled his divorce. He was also a man of letters who liked to discuss Flaubert and Proust. He had published small volumes of poetry not only in his native Córdoba but also in Buenos Aires when he lived there. Tall, corpulent but not quite sewn together, domineering, Carlos was very pleased to be again with his client.

"I want to show Barnstone and Alicia the city of Córdoba," Borges explained to Carlos. "You know, I have seventeeth-century ancestors who had something to do with the founding of this city."

Borges wrote a poem about the mythical founding of Buenos Aires, whose site was first glimpsed by Juan Díaz de Solís, an explorer looking for a passage to the Far East—an arrested ambition since, on rowing into the Rio de la Plata, Díaz de Solís was killed and eaten by Indians. Borges removes his native city from time and its founding:

To me it's mere fable that Buenos Aires had a beginning.
I feel it to be as eternal as the air and water.

We put our things in Carlos's car and sped away from the hotel and our money-hungry host. Carlos Alvarez had drunk a lot of wine at lunch. He had a distinct buzz as he toured us through the old city, by the statue of the founding conquistador, Cabrera y Cabrajal.

Borges said, "These were my names, Cabrera and Cabrajal. In those days justice was an easy matter. Justice was the sword. It was beautiful in battle, and justice and ethics were a question of who you were. If you were a conquistador, then horrendous massacres, bookburning, and razing of stone temples and cities were acts in service of God, king, and personal glory. You were an archetypal hero. Now, to be a general still usually means family, but it may also mean corruption, opportunistic Catholicism — I never understood Catholicism, my Catholicism; but then I don't like opera and bureaucracy — and justice in times like ours means torture, murder, and the most bestial human behavior. I'd say all the dubious progress of our century represents an improved conscience. At last we have tumbled many icons. We don't care for them anymore and do not stand in awe of them. Not to my credit, it took me a lifetime, I'm ashamed to say, not to feel respectful and intimidated by my own colonels, by my conquistadores, as when I wrote that portrait of Cabrera y Cabrajal. Those were years, much of my life, when I easily confused official bravery with bullying cowardice":

Conquistador

Carbrera and Cabrajal, these were my names.
I've drained the wineglass down to the last dram.
I've died and many times I've lived. I am
The Archetype. The others men. My claim:
For Spain and for the Cross I was the wan-
dering soldier. On unwalked lands and shores
Of an infidel continent I stirred up wars.
In fierce Brazil I carried the banner on.
Neither my king, nor Christ, nor the red gold
Were the instigating spur of all my bold-
ness that unleashed a terror in the wave
Of pagans. Yes, my justice was the sword
Handsome in bloody battle and its lord.
The rest? It doesn't matter. I was brave.

Unlike other Argentine cities, Córdoba has many colonial churches and houses. They are not rich and elaborate like those of Cuzco and Mexico City. (There was no gold in Argentina.) Their beauty is austere, as in the plain stone and wood walls of the Carmelite Convent of the Teresas or the residence of the Viceroy Sobremonte, with its bare patios containing a few old iron cannons, a fountain, and flowers whose brief, bright life always freshly contrasts with the old stone and wood. We passed the university, the site of the recent slaughter, and we went off to find the city gardens. A knight fell asleep under the willow tree in those gardens; when he woke, his maiden was gone. So he went back to sleep, unwilling to wake until he had her in his arms. He was buried there with his dream.

Suddenly Carlos woke to the hour. We set off, very fast, for the airport. I was suprised that Carlos was racing. We weren't that late, I thought.

I don't know how Borges knew, but he said to me, "Willis, I think Carlos is wrong. We are speeding off in the wrong direction. Perhaps he wants to take us to Tucumán."

"Or Patagonia."

We zipped out onto a country road as Carlos, betraying an expression of increasing strain, sought a familiar road sign. He increased speed as if this would guarantee our correct destination. Alicia, in the back, reached forward and grabbed my hand.

"Maybe, Willis, we will have the opportunity to miss the plane," said Borges, mischievous.

Alvarez hit the brakes, screeched almost to a halt, and Borges flew forward toward the windshield. I grabbed him by the left shoulder and we both hit the dashboard. Instead of stopping, our host pulled a U-turn and we roared off in the opposite direction.

"I've got a shortcut," he told us.

"Don't worry about the plane, Carlos," I cajoled. "You know Borges likes Córdoba. And especially your company. You were his good lawyer and friend, no?"

When he began to talk again, he slowed down measurably. I didn't think our death by accident was worth punctuality.

"Punctuality is the thief of time," Borges intoned. "That's Oscar Wilde. A clever man."

"Punctuality can also be the thief of life," I added.

"And a dreadful *waste* of time," joined in Alicia.

We were trying to convince our lawyer that we were really vagabonds who didn't give a damn about clocks, planes, or where we slept. Anything to slow him down. But the car lunged jerkily down the highway, as fast as he could push it. Finally we slowed and came rumbling over sand into the airport via an unorthodox entrance. Carlos jumped out and rushed us to the counter. Although he had been a most obliging and thoughtful host, he was now running. Borges wasn't very keen on jogging—and of course the plane was an hour late.

After we said goodbye to our friend, the good lawyer, we boarded the plane. Borges suddenly asked, "Where is my briefcase?"

I asked the attendant to hold the plane a minute. I got off, dashed back to the counter. There Carlos was still standing thoughtfully, with the nostalgic smile of important fellowship. I said a last farewell to him as I relieved him of Borges's briefcase, which he was holding serenely in his right hand.

"I feel like a track star," I said to Alicia and Borges as I reentered the cabin. "Do you think I should get off again and race the plane back to Buenos Aires?"

"Well, you would win, of course," Alicia assured me.

After our slaphappy race to the silver plane, we floated back to Buenos Aires, soothed by the quiet roar of the engines. I read poetry to Borges during most of the trip. Donne, Hopkins, Frost, Roethke. Borges got the idea for a poem from a comment I made on "Birches."

"That poem was Frost's impossible memory."

As we approached the city of the Rio de la Plata I began to read Gerard Manley Hopkins's "Terrible Sonnets." I observed that perhaps this was the first time that Hopkins' "Terrible Sonnets" had been read out loud on a plane from Córdoba to Buenos Aires. Yet really what else should one be doing while landing?

I wake and feel the fell of dark, not day.
What hours, O what black hours we have spent
This night! what sights you, heart, saw; ways you went!
And more must, in yet longer light's delay,
With witness I speak this. But where I say
Hours I mean years, mean life. And my lament
Is cries countless, cries like dead letters sent
To dearest him that lives alas! away.

In the city we dropped Alicia off first. As our taxi pulled up near Borges's house and I was paying the driver, the poet knew exactly where he was. He got out by himself, on the wrong side, lowering his head carefully. He found himself in the middle of the twilight street and tottered toward the sidewalk. It was extremely dangerous. As cars behind us were honking, he stood for an instant alone, helpless, undisturbed, waiting. By the time I got there he was at the curb, stepping up. He was tired from the trip, and a little proud of his perilous action.

At his door we rang the bell, but no one answered. Borges took out his key and turned the lock.

"The bolt is locked, so Fanny must be home," he said. "And she must be sleeping, since she didn't expect me till late evening. Here I am, returning to an empty house. I wonder why," he uttered grimly. "Please call me later tonight."

"Of course."

Fanny opened the door, yawning.

"How did it go?" she said, patting down his stray hair and straightening out his tie before he even got through the doorway.

"It was perfect," was his reply. "I gave a perfect lecture, didn't stumble or stutter once. I liked Córdoba, except that I had no chance to speak 'On Time.' We had problems with a madman."

"Borges, goodbye, and thanks for the good trip."

"You will come tomorrow, when I give my chat on Leopoldo Lugones. I want you to meet my old French cousin. You will like her face."

"I will come."

In the evening I was back in my pleasant cell. My friend Amanda Ortega, the photographer next door, wanted to see me. We talked a while. Her mother was dying, her Arabic-speaking Lebanese Maronite mother. Her father, a Spanish Jew from Syria, had died years earlier. Coming from an Arabic country, with three of her four grandparents Arabs, the Argentines called her *la turca* (the Turk), a usage also found in Mexico. Amanda helped me with my photography book. She had taken me one afternoon to the immense square, La Plaza de Mayo, filled with hundreds of thousands, where we heard Isabelita shouting into the microphone. I made an unfriendly remark about Perón. How could I not? His people had invented the category of the "disappeared" and Argentina was to continue its bloody days and nights of torture and killing.

"He wasn't good for Argentina, he gave the country away, he bankrupted it, he was a demagogue. But after all he did a few good things for the worker, and for whatever reason he concerned himself with the lower classes. In his speeches he addressed them as if they were important. No one else did it before, or would have."

Amanda taught me humility, even in regard to the Peróns, whose gangster regime was now murdering the Argentine people. I thought of those macho hoodlums that Borges painted so realistically—or fantastically and romantically. Were they all that much better than the thugs who kill the disappeared ones? Could some of those same *compraditos* from the barrios be, in other guises and missions, the very same killer thugs? Was their neighborhood mission, with its brutal methods, that different from the work of a national military police? Borges favored his red-haired *criollos* from the story "The Intruder," with their short-bladed daggers. He called them mean, feared, rustlers, cheats, responsible for several deaths and expansive only when drunk or gambling, which might be at the same time. Were they really admirable? What was noble about these roughnecks who shared the favors of Julia Burgos and killed her because she had become an object between them—killed her to save their own perhaps perverted friendship? Was Borges's mother right in disapproving of her gentle son's roughnecks, in despising them? Why is a knife fight impressive? I'm afraid it is for a story, for dramatic fiction, as are kidnapping, rape, and all the nice work of the regime. The ultimate spectacle is war. Each generation learns this.

When Amanda left a few hours later, I collapsed. No all-nighter that night. Before I slept, however, I considered this strange situation of my dedication to the old sage whose work and person had become a good part of my life, and would remain so. I'm not a hero worshiper, not particularly respectful of authority, of dignitaries and (ridiculous as the rhetoric seems) kings. (My first job—I was just twenty-one—was in a school for the Greek crown prince.) I just prefer to read, write, voyage, have friends, a lover. Yet here I was with Borges, who for me was the preeminent living writer. I have always felt at ease, even as a very young man, being with poets I esteemed enormously, the Spaniards Pedro Salinas and Vicente Aleixandre, the Greeks Angelos Sikelianos and George Seferis—now all dead. And here I was with Borges, half-father, half-child because of his dependence and marvelous inventive spirit, because of his child's *No* to the traditional world. To be "with Borges" was to be with Constantine Cavafy or Whitman or Sappho or San Juan de la Cruz or Wang Wei or Antonio Machado. There are more, but these, and Borges, are the poets to whom I have been closest. I learned more from the person Borges than from almost any book; yet, I repeat, the voice of the person and the voice on the page were the same. And if there had been no page, the person would remain the voice of literature, the sage, like "those few other sages who have been in the world," to use Luis de León's verse. Borges had become my "habit."

I was growing weary with my good fortune, and I crashed.

The Leopoldo Lugones lecture was excellent. I taped it. After the talk in an *instituto* in Buenos Aires, Borges was signing books. Then we went to the home of his cousin, a great lady his age, who had a natural French *r* in her Spanish. She had lived much of her life in Europe. I took a picture of her in the half-dark by pushing my film. It is dramatic, or she is dramatic, her mouth pursed, one eye in darkness, the other in your heart. White irregular dots on her black dress are her knight's jewelry. Her right hand protrudes from the picture (a two- by three-foot black-and-white portrait) like the jester in Rembrandt's Nightwatch which, when the old varnish was removed, turned out not to be a night march but an afternoon stroll. Her neck is seven rivers moving up to the delta of her gray face. In her one really visible eye are the circles, the fleck of island whiteness, and the interior planets.

Borges liked his cousin Sofia immensely. He was cheerful, and since he was with family he told us confidentially (surely to many others as well) how he had dictated the story "La intrusa" (The Intruder) to his mother. It appeared in 1966. His mother, Leonor, hated the plot and what it said about women, but she wrote it down accurately as he dictated. As he neared the end of the dictation, he paused. She continued writing.

"Now, it is done," his mother said.

"But I didn't give you the ending."

"No, but I wrote it."

"You wrote it?"

"No. I didn't write it. I copied down what you had not yet said. 'Today I killed her.' You had to write that. There was no other way. I copied out the ending."

Borges recounted the conversation and said, "My mother was right. I left the last lines of the conclusion exactly as she copied them out."

A few days later I ate alone with Borges.

"What has your blindness given you?"

"Maybe some memory, some hearing, and another sense of time. You remember my poem in "In Praise of Shadow." Di Giovanni insisted on calling it "In Praise of Darkness," and so the whole English edition of the book had an erroneous title. He didn't understand the condition of the blindman. We are not in darkness; we are in shadow."

Borges's shadow moved me. It was his condition—his aloneness, his meditation, his vision. At the same time, his shadow was his essential condition of affinity with the Spanish mystic of darkness, pain, serenity, and vision, San Juan de la Cruz.

"I see your lines about time becoming your Democritus," I said to him, " 'where you tear out your eyes in order to think,' and find the 'penumbra that is slow and gives no pain and flows along a slope near eternity.' They are John of the Cross's 'serene night of flame that burns and gives no pain.' Your slow penumbra is his serene night, and his night and your night burn and give no pain. John is always blind like you, living with no ray of light until he burns himself away in the light of his commingling. I don't want to compare more, but I see darkness—or shadow, if you prefer—as a condition of light, the necessary light, which is the secret center and what you are."

"You are entering my blindness."

"You gave it away."

After Christmas I went to Easter Island. *Holiday* magazine sent me there for a week. I had sent them a wire saying,

WISH DO STORY AND PHOTOGRAPHS CHRISTMAS ISLAND

By return wire came,

IF YOU MEAN EASTER ISLAND, ANSWER IS YES

Naturally, I meant Easter Island. They knew I meant Easter Island, and knew something about me.

I went. It was extraordinary. I immersed myself in it. I got drunk like the rest of the island on New Year's Eve, saw the Southern Cross as never before, talked to a beautiful Pascuense woman in her cave, and rode wild horses around the island. I saw fields of yams and sweet potatoes, Esso oil drums for roofs, and mammoth statues gazing at the ocean. I was distressed by Pablo Neruda's book about the island, which with lofty romance saw the abused colony as untouched paradise, without a word that his colonizing Chileans, of every government and period, did what they could to destroy the culture—its language, its writing system, its pagan religion. The Pascuenses (the people of Easter Island) live in tin shacks and caves, whereas the Chileans reside in urban houses. The island language cannot be spoken in the schools. I recorded the island's history of kidnapping, disease, and destruction on the basis of chonicles and sea captains' journals. And I enjoyed every moment of my stay.

Filled with all this adventure, I returned to Argentina, passing again through the twilight of Santiago, where the brave and maligned poet Nicanor Parra sat on Sunday mornings outside the Cathedral of Santiago, reading his poems, his hat beside him, with a sign asking for contributions for the "persecuted people and artists of Chile." When I reached Buenos Aires, Amanda's mother was dead. Borges was on a short trip to America and would not return before I had to leave. I would not see him in his Buenos Aires again. That Argentine autumn (our spring) saw the military oust Isabelita and install their own, even more bloody regime.

With all the richness I had found in Buenos Aires, all the friends, Argentina seemed in every way an empty country. Empty, but not like the "empty mountain" that gave Wang Wei his solitude, his transcendent silence.

Argentina was empty. Borges was gone.

When I Wake Up, I Wake
to Something Worse

> WB: What do you think of that momentary wakening,
> which is both exhilarating and frightening, of wondering
> how our minds happen to be thinking and talking? I always
> wake to the astonishment that I exist, that I am.
> BORGES: When I wake up, I wake to something worse.
> It's the astonishment of being myself.

WILLIS BARNSTONE: In case you want a hardboiled egg?

JORGE LUIS BORGES: Why, of course.

WB: And I'll crack it for you.

BORGES: Look here, if not, I can't break a hardboiled egg. Not a hard-boiled one!

WB: It's good to bring hardboiled eggs into radio stations, no?

BORGES: A fine combination, I feel. Hardboiled eggs and radio stations!

WB: Borges, would you put them in a poem?

BORGES: No, I wouldn't. Yet I suppose all things are right for a poem. All words are right. In fact, all things are. Anything can be done, you know, but very few things can be talked about.

WB: I have some questions. Maybe wordy, but your answers won't be.

BORGES: They will be laconic, yes?

WB: We know that consciousness resides in every other human being, yet we possess an awareness of only our own mind. At times we wake, as it were, to a puzzling knowledge of the mind's separate existence.

BORGES: Well, but this is a question on the nature of solipsism, no? Now, I don't believe in solipsism, because if I did I'd go mad. But of course it is a curious fact that we exist.

In April 1980, Borges and María Kodama were at Indiana University in Bloomington for three days of talks and commented readings. This conversation was recorded in the studio of WFIU, National Public Radio.

At the same time, I feel I am not dreaming you—or, let's put it the other way, that you are not dreaming me. But this fact of wondering at life may stand for the essence of poetry. All poetry consists in feeling things as being strange, while all rhetoric consists in thinking of them as quite common, as obvious. Of course I'm puzzled by the fact of my existing, of my existing in a human body, of my looking through eyes, hearing through ears, and so on. And maybe everything I have written is a mere metaphor, a mere variation on that central theme of being puzzled by things. In that case, I suppose, there's no essential difference between philosophy and poetry, since both stand for the same kind of puzzlement. Except that in the case of philosophy the answer is given in a logical way, and in the case of poetry you use metaphor. If you use language, you have to use metaphors all the time. Since you know my works (well, let the *word* go at that. I don't think of them as works, really), since you know my exercises, I suppose you have felt that I was being puzzled all the time, and I was trying to find a foundation for my puzzlement.

WB: In Cincinnati when an admirer said, "May you live one thousand years," you answered, "I look forward happily to my death." What did you mean by that?

BORGES: I mean that when I'm unhappy—and that happens quite often to all of us—I find a real consolation in the thought that in a few years, or in a few days, I'll be dead and then all this won't matter. I look forward to being blotted out. But if I thought my death was a mere illusion, that after death I would go on, then I would feel very, very unhappy. For, really, I'm sick and tired of myself. Now, of course if I go on and I have no personal memory of ever having been Borges, then in that case it won't matter to me because I may have been hundreds of odd people before I was born, but those things won't worry me, since I will have forgotten them. When I think of mortality, of death, I think of those things in a hopeful way, in an expectant way. I should say I am greedy for death, that I want to stop waking up every morning, finding: "Well, here I am, I have to go back to Borges."

There's a word in Spanish, I suppose you know. I wonder if it's any longer in use. Instead of saying to wake up, you say *recordarse,* that is, to record yourself, to remember yourself. My mother used to say *Que me recuerdas a las ocho,* "I want to be recorded to myself at eight." Every morning I get that feeling because I am more or less nonexistent. Then, when I wake up, I always feel I'm being let down. Because, well, here I am. Here's the same old stupid game going on. I have to be somebody. I have to be exactly that somebody. I have certain commitments. One of the commitments is to live through the whole day. Then I see all that routine before me, and all things naturally make me tired. Of course, when you're young you don't feel that way. You feel, well, I am so glad I'm back in this marvelous world. But I don't think I ever felt that way. Even when I was young. Especially when I was young. No, I have resignation. Now I wake up and I say: I have to face another day. I let it go at that. I suppose that people feel in different ways because many people think of immortality as a kind of happiness, perhaps because they don't realize it.

WB: They don't realize what?

BORGES: The fact that going on and on would be, let's say, awful.

WB: Would be another hell, as you say in one of your stories.

BORGES: Yes, it would be, yes. Since this life is already hell, why go in for more and more hell, for larger and larger doses!

WB: For two hundred years?

BORGES: Yes. Well, of course you might say that those two hundred years don't exist. For what really exists is the present moment. The present moment is being weighted down by the past and by the fear of the future. Really, when do we speak of the present moment? For the present moment is as much an abstraction as the past or the future. In the present moment you always have some kind of past, and some kind of future also. You are slipping all the time from one to the other.

WB: But obviously you have great moments of pleasure during your life.

BORGES: Yes, I suppose everybody has. But I wonder. I suppose those moments are perhaps finer when you remember them. Because when you're happy, you're hardly conscious of things. The fact of being conscious makes for unhappiness.

WB: To be conscious of happiness often lets in an intrusion of doubt.

BORGES: But I think I have known moments of happiness. I suppose all men have. There are moments, let's say, of love, riding, swimming, talking to a friend, let's say, conversation, reading, even *writing*—or, rather, not writing, but inventing something. When you sit down to write it, then you are no longer happy because you're worried by technical problems. But when you think out something, then I suppose you may be allowed to be happy. And there are moments when you're slipping into sleep, and then you feel happy, or at least I do. I remember the first time I had sleeping pills. (They were efficient, of course, since they were new to me.) I used to say to myself: Now hearing that tramway turn around the corner, I won't be able to hear the end of the noise it makes, the rumble, because I'll be asleep. Then I felt very, very happy. I thought of unconsciousness.

WB: Do you care about literary recognition? Do you want fame?

BORGES: No. No! Those things are nonexistent. At the same time, when it comes to me—and it may have come to me—I feel that I should be grateful. I mean if people take me seriously, I think, well, they are wrong. At the same time I should be thankful to them.

WB: Do you live for the next poem, story, or essay or conversation?

BORGES: Yes. Yes, I do.

WB: It seems to me that you're a lucky man to have unending obsessions to create and to record. Do you know why you had that destiny of being a writer? That destiny or that obsession?

BORGES: The only thing I know is that I need those obsessions. Because if not, why should I go on living? Of course, I wouldn't commit suicide, but I should feel very unjustified. This doesn't mean I think very much of what I write. It means that I *have* to write. Because if I don't write something and keep on being obsessed by it, then I have to write it and be rid of it.

WB: In the *Republic* Plato spends much time seeking a definition of justice, a kind of public definition. Is this notion valid to us personally? Is your life, which ends in death, a just experiment in life? Or is it a biological double-cross against both the mind and the body? Plato speaks about public justice. Given the fact of death, do you believe in private justice?

BORGES: I think the only justice is private justice. As to a public justice, I wonder if that really exists.

WB: Do you believe private justice exists? How do we consider morality and doomsday?

BORGES: At the very moment of our lives we know whether we're acting the right way or the wrong way. We might say that doomsday is going on all the time, that every moment of our lives we're acting wrongly or rightly. Doomsday is not something that comes at the end. It's going on all the time. And we know, through some instinct, when we have acted rightly or wrongly.

WB: Is there a biological treason in life because of death?

BORGES: I don't understand what you mean by biological double-cross. Biology sounds so dim to me, I wonder if I can take that word in, no?

WB: *Physical,* then.

BORGES: Well, *physical,* yes. I think I can understand that. I am a very simpleminded man. If you go in for those long fancy words, *biology* and *psychology.*

WB: We get into language that your father might have used, right?

BORGES: Yes, he might have used it, but he rarely did so, being a professor of psychology. A skeptic also.

WB: I spent one year of my life, when I was a student, seeking the center of consciousness. I never found it.

BORGES: I don't think you can. It keeps eluding you all the time.

WB: But I did discover that seeking oneself was fascinating and intolerable.

BORGES: Yes, it is. Of course, since I am blind, I have to do that more or less all the time. Before I went blind, I was always finding refuge in watching things, seeing things, in reading, while now I have to go in for thinking. Or, since my thinking capacity isn't too good, let's say for dreaming, and in a sense for dreaming away my life. That's the only thing I can do. Then of course I have to go in for long spells of loneliness, but I don't mind that. Before, I couldn't. Before, I remember I lived in a town called Adrogué south of Buenos Aires. When I went on a half-hour's journey and I had no book with me I felt very unhappy. But now I can spend hours and hours on end with no books, because I don't read them. And so I don't think of loneliness as being necessarily unhappy. Or, for example, if I get a spell of insomnia, I don't mind because time slips down. It's like an easy slope, no? So I just let myself go on living. When I was not blind, I always had to be furnishing my time with different things. Now I don't. I just let myself go.

WB: Yet you do very much enjoy all the times you are with others.

BORGES: But of course, I live in memory. And I suppose a poet should live in memory because, after all, what is imagination? Imagination, I should say, is made of memory and of oblivion. It is a kind of blending of the two things.

WB: You manage with time?

BORGES: Oh, yes. Everybody who goes blind gets a kind of reward: a different sense of time. Time is no longer to be filled in at every moment by something. No. You know that you have just to live on, to let time live you. That makes for a certain comfort. I think it is a great comfort, or perhaps a great reward. A gift of blindness is that you feel time in a different way from most people, no? You have to remember and you have to forget. You shouldn't remember everything because, well, the character I wrote about, Funes, goes mad because his memory is endless. Of course, if you forgot everything, you would no longer exist. Because you exist in your past. Otherwise you wouldn't even know who you were, what your name was. You should go in for a blending of the two elements, no? Memory and oblivion, and we call that imagination. That's a high-sounding name.

WB: I know, you don't go in for high-sounding words because you're a literary man.

BORGES: No, because I am too skeptical about words. A literary man hardly believes in words.

WB: To return to my original question: As I attempted to discover myself, it was fascinating and intolerable because the more profoundly I thought I had gone into myself, the more I disappeared until I was uncertain of everything, even of my own existence.

BORGES: Well, I think Hume said, When I've looked for myself, I have never found anybody at home. That's the way the world is.

WB: One goes from reverie to nightmare.

BORGES: I have a nightmare almost every night. I had one this morning. But it wasn't a real nightmare.

WB: What was it?

BORGES: It was this: I found myself in a very large building. It was a brick building. Many empty rooms. Large empty rooms. Brick rooms. Then I went from one to the other, and there seemed to be no doors. I was always finding my way into courtyards. Then after a time I was going up and down, I was calling out, and there was nobody. That large and unimaginative building was empty, and I said to myself: Why, of course, this is the dream of the maze. I won't find any door, so I'll just have to sit down in one of the rooms and then wait. And sometimes I wake up. And that actually happened. When I realized it and said, This is the nightmare of the maze, and since I knew all about it, I wasn't taken in by the maze. I merely sat down on the floor.

WB: And waited it out.

BORGES: I waited a moment and woke up.

WB: You have other recurrent nightmares? What are they?

BORGES: I have two or three. At this moment I think the maze is the one that comes back to me. Then I have another one, and that came out of my blindness. That is a nightmare of trying to read and of being unable to because the characters become alive, because every letter turns into other letters, and then the words at the beginning are short when I try to make them out. They are long Dutch words with repeated vowels. Or, if not, the spaces between the lines widen out, and then the letters are branching out. All that is done in black or red characters, on very glossy paper, and so large as to be intolerable. And when I wake up, those characters keep me company for some time. Then for a wild moment I think: I'll never be able to forget them and I'll go mad. That seems to be happening all the time. Especially after I lost my sight, I was having that dream of reading, of being unable to read because of the characters becoming alive. That is one of the dreams I have. And the others are dreams about mirrors, about masked people. I suppose I have three essential nightmares: the maze, the writing, and the mirrors. And then there are others that are more or less common to everybody, but those are my three recurrent nightmares. I have them almost every night. They stay with me for a minute or so after I'm awake. Sometimes they come before I'm quite asleep. Most people dream before going to sleep, and then they keep on dreaming a moment after they awake. They are in a kind of halfway house, no? Between waking and sleeping.

WB: It's also a place from which you gather much material for your writing, isn't it?

BORGES: Yes, it is. De Quincey and so on—there is a fine literary tradition to that. De Quincey must have worked out his nightmares when he wrote them down, no? Because they're so fine. Besides, they depend on words also. While nightmares, generally, don't depend on words. What's difficult about writing a nightmare is that the night-mare feeling does not come from the images. Rather, as Coleridge said, the feeling gives you the images.

WB: That's a major distinction, because most people think the opposite. They don't think it all through.

BORGES: When you write down the images, those images may not mean anything to you. It's what you get in the case of Poe and of Lovecraft. The images are awful but the feeling isn't awful.

WB: And I suppose a good writer is one who comes up with the right images to correspond to the feeling.

BORGES: To a feeling, yes. Or who may give you the nightmare feeling with common objects or things. I remember how I found a proof of that in Chesterton. He says that we might think that at the end of the world there is a tree whose very shape is evil. Now that's a fine word, and I think that stands for that kind of feeling, no? Now, that tree could hardly be described. While, if you think of a tree, for example, made of skulls, of ghosts, that would be quite silly; but what he said, a tree *whose very shape is evil.* That shows he really had a nightmare about that tree. No? If not, how would he know about that tree?

WB: I've always been puzzled why my tongue moves, why words come out of my mouth or from in my head. These words are like seconds of a clock, happening, sounding almost by themselves.

BORGES: But I think that before going to sleep you begin, at least I begin, to mumble meaningless sentences. And then I know that I am going to sleep. When I hear myself, when I overhear myself saying something meaningless, it's a good sign that I'll be asleep in a moment.

WB: Well, I was going to ask you about the words happening, forming in our mouths. As long as time exists, the words come. Hence also the thoughts. But I don't will those words, or even will to will them. They possess me.

BORGES: I don't think those words stand for any meaning. At least you don't know the meaning.

WB: I don't mean the words before one sleeps. I mean all the words that are coming to you right at this moment, or to me. In other words, I don't know why words are coming out of my mouth right now. Some force is letting them out. I am never there manipulating them. I don't understand that; it's a fundamental mystery to me.

BORGES: But I suppose those words go with certain thoughts. Otherwise they would be meaningless or irrelevant.

WB: But I feel like a clock wound up in which the seconds tick, in which words come. I have no idea why I'm speaking to you in any half-logical way now. Or why you're answering me. It's a tremendous puzzle.

BORGES: Yes. I think you should accept that.

WB: I do accept it or I'd go mad.

BORGES: Yes, that's it. You might even say that if you try to *think*, you go mad.

WB: Yes.

BORGES: Thought should be carefully avoided, right?

WB: Well, if you try to think why you think, you can't think that. Yet sometimes I walk down the street and say, not Who is this walking down the street, but Who is this thinking he's walking down the street? And then I'm really puzzled.

BORGES: Yes, and then you go on to thinking who is this thinking he's thinking he's thinking, no? I don't think that stands for anything. That's merely grammatical, they are only words.

WB: It sounds like a mirror.

BORGES: You might go into a second category. You may feel a very strong physical pain. For example, you may get it through electricity or through a toothache. Then when you feel that pain, you won't feel the pain. Then after that you say, well, this is a toothache, and then you know that you felt the pain. Then after that you might go for a third time and say, well, I knew that I knew. But after that I don't think you can go on. You can do it successfully within the same game, because you keep on thinking the same thing over and over again. But I don't think you could do that any more than three times over. If you say, I think that I think that I think that I think that I think that I think, all of that is quite unreal after the second term, perhaps. I read a book, by John William Dunne, *Experience with Time*, in which he says that since, if you know something, you know that you know it, and you know that you know that you know, and you know that you know that you know that you know it, then there is an infinity of selves in every man. But I don't think that can be proved.

WB: What do you think of that momentary wakening, which is both exhilarating and frightening, of wondering how our minds happen to be thinking and talking? I always wake to the astonishment that I exist, that I am.

BORGES: When I wake up, I wake to something worse. It's the astonishment of being myself. So and so born in Buenos Aires in 1899, somebody who was in Geneva.

WB: Why aren't you the Peking Man, or someone who's going to live five million years from now?

BORGES: Well, once I thought out a kind of fantasy, which was for literary purposes. This is that at any moment we all change into somebody else. Now, since you are changed into someone else, you are not aware of it. For example, at some moment I will be changed into you. You will be changed into me. But since the change, the shift, is complete, you have no memories; you don't know that you are changing. You're changing all the time. You may be the man in the moon, yet you will not know about it, since, when you became the man in the moon, you became the man in the moon with *his* past, with his memories, with his fears, with his hopes, and so on.

WB: The past self is obliterated.

BORGES: Yes. You may be changed into somebody else all the time and nobody would know. Maybe that kind of thing is happening. It would be meaningless, of course. It reminds me of a story, only a story, but things are only good for literary purposes! But for not too good literary purposes, for trick stories.

WB: There is a powerful force, always in us, to move out from ourselves to reach the world. It shows itself in all ways: sexually, by writing, by talking, by touching —

BORGES: Well, living.

WB: By living. We are only ourselves, and yet there exists the strongest impulse to destroy our solitude by including more in it. Sappho has a fragment where she sums it up: "I could not hope/ to touch the sky/ with my two arms." Even if she can't — her aspiration is to embrace the sky.

BORGES: If I understand you, you say that we're running away from ourselves all the time, and that we have to do so.

WB: We're trying to expand to be more, to reach, to touch outside our own circle.

BORGES: I suppose we are. But I don't think you should worry about that. You should not feel unhappy about that. Even though you know we can't do it, or can't do it utterly, only in an imperfect way.

WB: We cannot do it, but part of the art of living is to go through the motions of doing it. It makes for writing, it makes for love, it makes for all the things that bind people together.

BORGES: Since we're given — what? — threescore years and ten, and we have to furnish them somehow, why not attempt those things? And after all, we have a life span. If not, you'd be utterly bored.

WB: You obviously value your future work as more important than earlier achievements.

BORGES: Well, I have to.

WB: Anything less would be fatal. Yet I'm surprised that you seem to consider your recent books of poems less important than earlier books of poems.

BORGES: I know them only too well.

WB: I'm convinced that your new poems are your most powerful, in both their intelligence and their passion. The latter is often expressed in a personal despair that you do not allow in your stories or essays.

BORGES: No, I think you are wrong. You think of my poems as being good. You read them through the light of the early poems, but had these poems come to your notice as being the work of an unknown poet, you'd toss them away. Don't you think so? When you read something written by a writer whose work you know, then you read those last pieces as the last pages in a long novel, but those pages would make no sense without the pages that came before them. When you think of a poet, you always tend to think of his last poem as a fine poem, but taken by itself it may not be.

WB: Yes, but the last poems also help the early poems because they contribute to the cumulative personality of the voice. Without those last poems your earlier poems would be heard less fully.

BORGES: Well, I suppose they are helping each other.

WB: Because they create one total voice. When Blake says something amusing, it's partly amusing because usually he doesn't say anything amusing, and therefore we say: Ah, there's Blake being witty in an epigram.

BORGES: He's generally long-winded and ponderous!

WB: To me your new poems are your most powerful in terms of intellect and passion.

BORGES: Let's hope so. I don't think of them in that way. They are mere exercises. Besides, as I feel lonely for something, I feel homesick, those poems are merely experiments in being back in Buenos Aires or in running away from things. They are merely meant to be used for padding the new book I'm writing. But I do hope you're right.

WB: As you stand before a mirror or record a dream in the poems, your precise delineation of pathos is a quality lost to modern poetry.

It is well that you do not overesteem your recent poems, but you should know that you're probably wrong in your judgment.

BORGES: But I hope I'm wrong! I'm glad to be convinced by you, only I can't. I don't want to be right. Why should I be right? Why should I insist on the fact that I'm writing very poor stuff?

WB: Is there a poem usually lurking in your mind that you stumble on? Is it an act of recognition of a common thing, as when you suddenly remember that you love your mother or father? Is it that you fall upon a poem, or does the poem fall on you?

BORGES: I would say the poem falls on me, and even more in the case a short story. Then I am possessed. Then I have to get rid of it, and the only way to get rid of it is to write it down. There is no other way of doing so, or else it keeps on.

WB: You say your poems are mere exercises, but what are they exercises in?

BORGES: I suppose they are exercises in language. They are exercises in the Spanish language, in the euphony of verse, exercises in rhyming so. Since I'm not too good a rhymer, I try to get away with it. And they are also exercises in imagination.

In the case of a story, I know that I must think out a story, clearly and coherently, and then I can write it down. If not, I can't. If not, the whole thing would be a jumble of words. It should be more than that. A story should mean not only the words but something behind the words.

I remember reading—maybe it was one of Stevenson's essays: "What is a character in a book? A character in a book is merely a string of words," he said. Now, I think that's wrong. He may be a string of words, but he should not leave us the impression of being a string of words. Because when we think of Macbeth or Lord Jim or Captain Ahab, we think of those characters as existing beyond the written words. We are not told everything about them, but there are many things that have happened to them that surely existed. For example, we are told about a character doing such and such a thing. Then the next day he does another thing. Now, the writer doesn't say anything about it. We feel that he had his nights of sleep, that he has had his dreams, that things happened to him that we are not being told about. We think of Don Quijote as having been a child, though there is not a word concerning Don Quijote's childhood in the book, as far as I remember. So the character should be more than a string of words. And if he is not more than words, he should not be a real character. You wouldn't be interested in him. Even in the case of a character who exists, let's say, within ten lines: "Alas, poor Yorick, I knew him well, Horatio." That character exists by himself. Yet he only exists as a string of words within ten lines, or perhaps even less.

WB: And in someone else's mouth. He never even presents himself on stage.

BORGES: Yes, in someone else's mouth. And yet you think of him as having been a real man.

WB: And feel compassion for him.

BORGES: And feel compassion for him. Shakespeare had Hamlet in a graveyard. He thought that making him handle a skull, a white skull—Hamlet was in black—all that would have made a quite effective picture. But since he couldn't be holding the skull and not saying a word, he had to say something. And so Yorick came into being through that technical necessity of Shakespeare's. And he came into being forever. In that sense Yorick is far more than a string of words. I suppose Stevenson knew all that, since he was a writer, since he created many characters, and those characters were far more than a string of words.

WB: And in ten words he outsmarts time forever.

BORGES: Yes. That's very strange, eh?

WB: I have a very personal question.

BORGES: The only interesting questions are personal questions. Not those of the future of the Republic, the future of America, the future of the cosmos! These things are meaningless.

WB: I think these questions have all been rather personal.

BORGES: They should be personal.

WB: Do you have paternal feelings toward your friends? Or is this word *paternal* completely irrelevant?

BORGES: No, they're not paternal.

WB: Everyone is an equal?

BORGES: Brotherly; fraternal, rather than paternal. Of course, being an old man I'm expected to be paternal, but really I'm not. Now, Macedonio Fernández thought that paternal feelings were wrong. He said to me, "What do I have in common with my son? We belong to different generations. I'm fond of him, but that's my mistake. He's fond of me, that's his mistake. We shouldn't really care for each other."

Then I said to him: "Yes, that doesn't depend on the rule. You may care for him in spite of those arguments. And suppose your arguments are made because you think you are worrying too much over him, or you feel that you haven't done right by him. There's quite a lot of nonsense about fathers not being allowed to love their sons and sons not being allowed to love their fathers."

WB: Go on.

BORGES: Of course, he had abandoned his family. There's a very obvious explanation: the fact that he had left them to live his own life.

WB: To go from fathers to reverie, you speak much of dream. What do you mean by dream? How is a dream different from any other state of wakefulness?

BORGES: Because a dream is a creation. Of course, wakefulness may be a creation: part of our solipsism and so on. But you don't think of it in that way. In the case of a dream, you know that all that comes from yourself, whereas, in the case of a waking experience, many things may come to you that don't come out of yourself, unless you believe in solipsism. Then you are the dreamer all the time, whether waking or sleeping. I don't believe in solipsism; I don't suppose anybody really does. The essential difference between the waking experience and the sleeping or dreaming experience must lie in the fact that the dreaming experience is something that can be begotten by you, created by you, evolved out of you.

WB: But not necessarily in sleep.

BORGES: No, no, not necessarily in sleep. When you're thinking out a poem, there is little difference between the fact of being asleep and that of being awake, no? And so they stand for the same thing. If you're thinking, if you're inventing, or if you're dreaming, then the dream may correspond to vision or to sleep. That hardly matters.

WB: Like all of us, you are a selfish man. You have dwelled on yourself, have explored and exploited your own mind, and have transmitted your observations to others.

BORGES: Well, what else can I do? I shouldn't be blamed, I shouldn't be held to blame for that.

WB: Because you have transmitted your self-observations to others, you are surely not selfless. Yet the fact of giving your work to others, as you also offer a kind of Socratic conversation to others, is an act of generosity of a curiously rare ethical breed.

BORGES: I think I need it, because I'm enjoying it also.

WB: Yet I fear this breed of ethical generosity is becoming extinct. One like you, protected by blindness and loyalty to earlier authors, may not appear again. Then I worry a bit more and become optimistic and think that this ethical man and artist will occur again.

BORGES: He or she will be lost forever and ever!

WB: Are you an ethical man?

BORGES: Yes, I am essentially ethical. I always think of things in terms of right and wrong. I think that many people in my country, for example, have little feeling for ethics. I suppose in America people are more ethical than in my country. People here, for example, generally think of a thing as being right or wrong, the war in Vietnam, and so on. In my country you think of something as being profitable or un-profitable. That may be the difference. But here Puritanism, Protestant-ism, all that makes for ethical considerations, while the Catholic religion makes for pomp and circumstance only — that is, for essential atheism.

WB: There's a lot of fun in you, Borges. You're very childlike, you enjoy things, you have tremendous humor.

BORGES: Well, I should, after all. I wonder if I'm really grown up. I don't suppose anybody is.

WB: No, none of us is. When I was unhappy in the past, in love, some foolish things like that —

BORGES: No, not foolish. Those things are a part of every human experience. I mean, the fact of loving and not being loved, that is a part of every biography, no? But if you came to me and said: I am in love with so-and-so, she's rejected me — I think that every human being can say that. Everyone has been rejected, and has rejected also. Both things stand out in everyone's life. Someone is turning down someone or being turned down. It's happening all the time. Of course, when it happens to us, as Heine said, then we're very unhappy.

WB: Sometimes when I was unhappy I wanted to die, but I knew this was just a sign that I wanted to live.

BORGES: I have thought of suicide many times, but I've always put it off. I say, why should I worry, since I have that very powerful weapon, suicide. And at the same time I never used it — at least I don't *think* I ever used it!

WB: Well, you've almost answered my question. I wanted to say that the thought of suicide was merely a sign of wanting to live, that even the false suicide I often conceived was a desperate wish to live more fully, better.

BORGES: When people think of suicide, they only think of what people will think about them knowing that they committed suicide. So in a sense they go on living. They do it out of revenge, generally speaking. Many people commit suicide because they are angry. It is a way of showing their anger and revenge. To make someone else guilty for what you do, which is remarkably wrong.

WB: Suicide is largely a young man's romance, a false door young people sometimes step into. But what about the converse? Why the passion to live? Why that passion that drives the young to death and the writer to his pen? Why the consuming passion to live?

BORGES: If I could answer that, I could explain the riddle of the universe, and I don't think I can, no? Since everybody else has failed. I've known many suicides. Many of my friends have committed suicide. In fact, among literary men in my country, suicide is fairly common, perhaps more than in this country. But I think that most of them have done it out of a desire to spite somebody, to make somebody guilty of their own death. In most cases that is the motivation. In the case of Leopoldo Lugones, I think he was trying to turn somebody else into a murderer.

WB: Sometimes there's a weariness, a desire to be released, when people are very sick.

BORGES: Of course there's another kind of suicide. When a friend of mine knew he had a cancer, he committed suicide, which was a reasonable thing to do. I wouldn't hold that against anybody. I think that it was right.

WB: I don't have any more questions unless you have a question you'd like to ask me.

BORGES: No, I would like to thank you for your kindness and for this very pleasant conversation, because I thought of it as an ordeal, and it hasn't been an ordeal. On the contrary, it has been a very pleasant experience. You were very generous to be feeding me, giving me your own thoughts, pretending that I really thought them out. You've done everything, been handling me very deftly all the time, and I'm very grateful to you. Thank you, Barnstone.

WB: Thank you, Borges.

What Seneca Said
in a Chicago Taxi

"Perhaps I am terrified. But I don't think I am afraid, and
I do welcome death. But not today, in our company, with
you beside me, and María a few seats back. Perhaps, some
day in Buenos Aires, when I feel particularly alone, and it is
raining. Rain is a good time for sadness, as you know from
the sentimental poets."

Borges and María were to arrive on an early spring day in
New York from Buenos Aires. I was to be with them for most of a
month. We'd been speaking on the phone from continent to continent,
making arrangements, but no business call went by without being
quickly overcome by literature or by the most recent curious incident
of his life in Buenos Aires. Then a wire came, giving the date of
their arrival in New York, signed BORGES.

The day was sunny and happy. I arrived at Kennedy International
Airport early, unusual for me. I was living that year, 1980, in Brooklyn,
in Cobble Hill near the Bridge. The plane was an hour late, having
made an unscheduled stop in Santiago de Chile. No sooner was the
plane parked against its silver cocoon than it emptied immediately.
The passengers walked out in twos, in triumph. I waited until the
very last laggard had come through the gate. I asked the attendant if
there were others or whether there was another plane.

"There's no one left on the plane," came the authoritative answer.

Tomorrow, I thought. I was desolate. I lingered about twenty minutes some thirty feet from the exit, looking in all directions. Then —
not in the direction of the plane, but from behind — I turned and
saw María, and Borges sitting grandly in a wheelchair. His smile was
as big as the sky. I was upset at seeing him in a wheelchair — had it
been that long? — but I soon realized the chair was for his blindness,
not his health.

"María! Borges!"

"It's a year since we were last together?" Borges said.

"No, it's four."

"It feels like a year," he insisted.

"How's the original Saint James?" I asked. "Do they still give you that nice seat by the mirrors and serve you hot chocolate at midnight so you can keep on chatting?"

"They go on being polite and kind to their good customer, this old man."

"Welcome to the Saint James Infirmary Blues," I told him.

Borges was on his feet. I don't remember why, but I was confiding in his ear a few lines from one of Quevedo's great poems that starts *La vida empieza en lágrimas y caca* (A life begins with tears and turds). Borges continued the verses. We were back at the beginning. (What could have happened if, thinking they were not on the plane, I had left the airport, and they were there alone? What a thought!)

From his memory pouch Borges pulled out the right song lyrics for our particular city of Saint James.

Let her go, let her go, God bless her,
Wherever she may be.
She can look at the whole wide world all over
She'll never find another man like me.

Now when I die I want you to dress me in straight laced
    shoes,
A bossback coat and a Stetson hat.
Put a 20-dollar gold piece on my watchchain
So the boys will know I die standing pat.

"*Vamos al pueblo.* Let's go into town," I said.

"You know, María," Borges observed, "only a few hours ago we left the autumn in Argentina. And look here, in New York, without thinking, it's spring."

The moon can't know it is serene and clear,
Nor can it even know it is the moon.

Off for the luggage. Old rockingchair hadn't got Borges. In high spirits, full of wit and energy, he took María by the arm and caned happily into the New York early afternoon.

That evening we were crossing the Brooklyn Bridge. I had picked up my car at my place on Sackett Street; we were on our way to

Manhattan, where Borges and María would sleep. The next day we'd
be in Chicago—Carl Sandburg's city, Borges called it—where we were
to have a talk before a graduate audience at the University of Chicago.
As we left Walt Whitman's city, Brooklyn, heading for Washington
Irving's town, Manhattan, Borges sensed a historic moment of great
import. We were on the Brooklyn Bridge, the bridge of Hart Crane, of
Mayakovski, of Garcia Lorca—all, like himself, foreigners to the city,
who had resided there and written of its revelation. Borges noted,
"Manhattan's skyscrapers soar upward like jets of water."

When we had crossed over, he said, "Barnstone, do you mind if
we go over the bridge once again?"

As we rolled at the bottom of the bridge, down the confusing
streets of Chinatown, I turned and headed back to Brooklyn. In
Brooklyn we passed the Jehovah's Witness dwarf skyscraper, with its
neon message on top aimed to God and the apostles. We turned once
more, and I slowed the car almost to a walking pace. Borges, with
reverence, recited from Hart Crane's "Proem: To Brooklyn Bridge":

> How many dawns, chill from his rippling rest
> The seagull's wings shall dip and pivot him,
> Shedding white rings of tumult, building high
> Over the chained bay waters Liberty—

"Strange how a man who wrote about the 'choiring strings' of that
'harp and altar' could drop into the same waters, in a desperate
moment, or maybe a meaningless moment—Katherine Anne Porter
said he was drunk earlier in the evening—and drown. I think he
wrote his best poems in Mexico, those rushed fragmentary poems,
but he seemed to know his moment was brief, 'an instant in the
wind.' He wrote 'The Broken Tower' there."

Borges reached again into his memory bank, and from it read a
stanza from his "Tower":

> And so I entered the broken world
> To trace the visionary company of love, its voice
> An instant in the wind (I know not whither hurled)
> But not for long to hold each desperate choice.

I dropped María and Borges off at their Park Avenue apartment,
which Dutton publishers had found for them. The next morning we
were on the plane to Chicago.

Flying with Borges is not a simple experience. He claimed that he didn't enjoy being lost in those big metal birds. Small planes are better. I do recall his beaming look as he stepped out of the little prop engine grasshopper on a spring day in Bloomington. He descended the stairs with one arm stretched to the sky. He stopped, turned his head upward, his eyes laughing brightly as they scanned the sky. As if he were having a mystical experience, he uttered the words, "It smells of corn!"

Borges said he preferred the smaller planes because he could feel the sense of flight, be part of it. The big ones made him feel diminished and apart. In the many air trips I took with him, he was, even more than in walks around a city, given to conversation that knew no pause. Since there were no obstacles—no streets to cross, no noises, no passersby shaking his hand; just space outside, silent to our ears—the plane provided another kind of intimacy and obligation. As always, Borges was incapable of uttering a sentence that was not memorable or worthy of a book. But Borges, so given to books, to libraries, which were his infinite mirrors of history, knew the dialogic difference between speech and print. Speech was alive and bookfree. The great figures of discourse, the foremost ones who gave us our Eastern and Western religions, wrote nothing.

"What are you working on these days?" I asked.

"Well, I would like to do a book on Angelus Silesius. But he has already entered a short story, and maybe that's the best I can do. Nevertheless, María and I are working on it." His face glowed.

"Borges, I suspect you like to write, since I see that when we talk about those things your face takes on a beam of smug virtue."

"I'll take out my mirror and check up on you to see if I really have such a glow. If so, I will be more careful. Yet better a beam of virtue than a shadow of sin."

"You have the real makings of a formal sinner. I also suspect you would have soon been tied to the stake for a hot auto-da-fé in an earlier century in any country that had respectable standards of thought and behavior."

"But I have *tried* to be a proper heretic. I think I have failed at this too, however, for lack of originality, as I have failed at every endeavor."

"You are clearly a *fracasado,* a man of weakness who has drifted with every easy current of wind."

"You've taken my words from me."

"I apologize."

Borges turned the tables on me. Here I found myself apologizing, as if I were Borges, proclaiming my modesty.

"Let me ask you a personal question, Barnstone."

"I thought all questions were personal. But I also thought you were disinterested in personal small talk as were, you said, your Japanese hosts all the time you were in Japan. But go ahead."

We had been talking nonstop for an hour since fastening ourselves into the seat belts. Because I was sitting twisted fully toward him, with exhausting and exhilarating attention, the muscles in my abdomen cramped, as if I were in frozen water. They turned into ice. I said nothing.

"What time do we arrive in Chicago?" he asked.

"Sometime after you ask your question."

"What do you think of María?" he asked, seriously and confidentially.

"I've told you before. You are not worthy of her." I wasn't going to let him get away with such infamy.

"I'm very pleased to see you've found me out—and more, that you appreciate María."

"It's not hard to do either. Of course I appreciate María. Do you think I'm blind? She's wonderful."

"I also think this. But, look here, sometimes I am aware that she needs to be free of this old man's company. She has been trying to go to Japan. I told her I would be glad to go with her and die in Japan. I'm not sure it made her happy. It was a joke, of course."

"Yes, sometimes jokes are the only truths we utter."

"You win," he said. "I capitulate to you and Freud, who is not my favorite fiction writer."

"Do you mind if I ask you a more difficult personal question?"

"Of course. Are there real questions between people that are not personal? The others are chatter and formal superstitions."

"It's in regard to death. You speak so often about your disbelief in God, in afterlife, of a death that you welcome, for which you are ready at any time. At the same time you speak as a young man with a 'promising career,' saying you don't care about your own earlier books, don't care to reread them or even to own them, and think only about the new ones you are planning to write. Because of all these contradictions—at least I think them contradictions—I wonder whether, instead of welcoming death, you are not terrified by it? Maybe you are courageous. Like that Socrates whom you praised for drinking down the hemlock, as opposed to the Jesus who called out from the cross. I wonder if you are not both courageous and terrified, since the two go together?"

"Perhaps I am terrified. But I don't think I am afraid, and I do welcome death. But not today, in our company, with you beside me, and María a few seats back. Perhaps, someday in Buenos Aires, when I feel particularly alone, and it is raining. Rain is a good time for sadness, as you know from the sentimental poets."

"In my college days when I took a math course, about all I remember is that zero and infinity were being substituted for each other as equals in order to make a problem in trigonometry or calculus turn out. Is it possible that death and immortality are interchangeable?"

"Why, yes. But if death and immortality are interchangeable, it means simply that immortality means eternal darkness. For others that is not very desirable. For me it is fine. Therefore I believe in immortality, at least the kind for which you have given me the formula."

In his autobiographical reflections Anthony Kerrigan observed how, on the question of non-being, Borges found his typical formula of reversal: "Borges was obsessed with oblivion, just as Unamuno, his immediate predecessor in these matters, was obsessed with everlastingness. In the same Hispanic way, Borges longed for the obverse of eternity, nothingness" (Kerrigan, "Autobiography," 211).

"Willis, in this plane I feel a sense of intimacy as when the cat is let out of the bag and it doesn't matter. Of course, my bottom is a little sore and here I am strapped in, but that slight hum of the motor outside and the hum of voices inside give us a little room, just you and I. What do you think of love for a woman?"

"I am in favor of the habit," I said, astonished.

"I'm in favor of friendship," he retorted.

"Yes, I know."

"That's why I'm interested in love for a woman, meaning, after Adam and Eve left their dream in the Garden and entered the time of the stubborn clock, we have love, death, and friendship. And as Paul said, or should have said, the finest of these is friendship. So what do you think of remembering love?"

"Better to remember than not to have remembered at all," I told him, pompously.

"I'm an old skeptical man, with a twentieth-century disdain for the sentimental, though you know I'm also a literary anachronism, and with all that sometimes I feel like one of those symbolist or decadent poets, my much disdained Baudelaire of the isles and the mistresses or Verlaine, the man of music, drunk with gardens of statues and fountains, and a woman lurking there poised like a beautiful landscape."

"Borges, I suspect you of being Adam newly released from Paradise, on a frantic hunt for erotic memories. I'm so happy to see you acting a bit indecently."

"My future is as certain as irregular rain. But I do retain some dreams of real women which did not remain wholly dreams."

"There's one sitting behind us, if you had any damn eyes in your head."

"This is a good little room, isn't it?"

"Yes, one made cunningly."

Our conversation seemed to be a second act of that memory of his own Adam, the one he liked, the one cast out who had therefore the possibility and shabby gleam of real love in the slow but incessant time on the earth, who is consoled:

Adam Cast Forth

Was there a Garden or was the Garden dream?
Slowly in my vague light, today I've asked,
Almost as consolation, if the past,
Of which this Adam, in his shabby gleam
Of misery now, was master once, or was
It slander of that God I dreamt. My eyes
Have no clear memory now of Paradise,
And yet I know that it exists and does
Persist, though not for me. The stubborn clock
Of earth's my punishment, incestuous fray
And war of Cains and Abels and their flock.
Yet, notwithstanding, to have loved is much,
To have been happy, long ago to touch
The living Garden, even for a day.

At O'Hare we were met by Marjorie Pannell, a smart, lovely graduate student at the University of Chicago. As we drove through the city, spring was almost palpably in the air. We stopped first at Stuart Brent's bookstore, and Borges sat pleased amid the books. Then it was time to head toward the university. In the taxi Marjorie and María sat on jump seats; Borges and I were deep in the heavy black leatherette seat behind. Borges liked contact with the people wherever we were, but of course, being blind, he was often a little shy — though sometimes not at all, especially if someone else began a conversation. Then he would chat with whoever was there, student or stranger, with the same fervor and candor as with an old friend. For a man of such gentlemanly and old-fashioned decorum, he was always quite ready to accept every unknown voice that ventured to address him.

"You from Chicago?" I asked the driver.

"Nah. I just work in this dump. What about you guys?"

"Borges and Miss Kodama are from Argentina. Marjorie is from Boston. I'm from Indiana."

"Well, you're the one from the boonies. Hey, buddy, I was in Europe too. You been there?"

The driver was about sixty, a little plump under his light checkered polyester jacket. Over his dashboard was a bluish picture of the Virgin Mary. His voice had the city music of a good snarling rasp.

"When were you in Europe?" I asked, "What'd you do there?"

"Just a soldier. In the war," he said, laconically.

"Did you see action?"

"Yeah. O'course I seen action. I was infantry. Went in four days after D Day."

"What was it like?"

"Listen, buddy. I'm sorry. I was the one started talkin' about it. But I don't talk about what I seen."

"You mean . . ."

"I mean, I don't talk about what really happened, because I don't think about it." His voice dropped and he paused.

"Why don't you think about what really happened?" I insisted.

I was pushing, but the driver was into our squabble. I liked to draw people out when I was with Borges, and this time I had a good feeling. Instinctively I liked the driver.

"You want to know. OK. I know you guys want to get me to talk about it. I don't mind. I'll give you the whole goddamn poop in three or four words. I don't think about the war, about all those things of the past, because memory is hell."

Borges seized my wrist. In a low, urgent voice he said to me, "This man has been a solider. He has known bitterness. He has known unhappiness and now he hates memory. *Memory is hell. Memory is hell.* Why, those words could have been written by Seneca."

Borges informed our hosts at the University of Chicago of the driver's declaration about hell and memory. It was clear that this incident and the three sententious words, the Senecan maxim, had entered his own memory, along with other significant readings and earlier experiences. It was only later that I remembered one of his sonnets, "Ewigkeit" (Eternity), in which he speaks of Seneca's horrendous words and confirms that if there is one thing he cannot escape, it is memory: the memory of our destiny as worms and ash and of the good things too — a blacksmith forge, the moon, the evening mist. The latter are lost on earth but persist in eternity, where memory keeps them:

Ewigkeit

Let me turn over in my mouth a verse
In Spanish to confirm what Seneca
In Latin always says: his horrid curse
Declaring that the world's a formula
For worms. Let me sing out his pallid ash,
The calendars of death and victory
Of that bombastic queen who tries to smash
And stomp the banners of our vanity.
Enough of that. What may have blessed my dust
I'm not a fool and coward to deny,
And know there is one thing that can't exist:
Forgetting. Yet the precious things I've lost
Endure, burn in eternity: the sky
And moon, the blacksmith forge, the evening mist.

The format of the *charla* before an audience largely of graduate students was for Ricardo Gullón, a Spanish scholar, to introduce us. Borges and I were to be chatting. Borges spoke warmly about the cold city. Immediately he captivated the audience. The students in turn gave that darkish auditorium the cheerful illumination of quick minds enjoying the colloquy.

I must report an incident that took place in an instant, that afternoon in 1980. It was minor and passing, but it gives balance to what otherwise might seem to be unrelieved euphoria.

Background. For many years I have been interested in women's poetry. In 1962 I published a book of Sappho's poems in Greek, with a translation and study. My daughter, Aliki, and I did a large anthology called *A Book of Women Poets from Antiquity to Now.* I regularly teach a course in women poets for Indiana's women's studies program, for which I am a faculty member. More recently I published a book called *Sappho and the Greek Lyric Poets.* These are signs of a preoccupation with women's poetry, most of which began three decades earlier, when universities did not yet have women' studies programs. In other words, the signs say I lack a history as an insensitive sexist.

In our conversation that afternoon, I said to Borges, "Thinking of yourself as a medieval Everyman, what would you say about. . . ." As soon I had uttered the word "Everyman," a loud hiss filled the auditorium. It was a buzzword and had to be hissed. The proper word was *Everyperson,* which Borges would not have understood as the medieval personage. I got my comeuppance. Borges looked puzzled. I was a little flustered and tense, tried not to be, not wishing to hurt the flow. I had not been publicly hissed before and, being an adventurer, I look at all experience as interesting. We moved on and that was it—but Seneca spoke, instructing and warning me too, from the floor of the Chicago auditorium.

After the talk we hired a limo to take us back to Bloomington, about four and a half hours south. Borges was in a great mood, talking about Alfonso Reyes, the Mexican essayist who had been his friend and early champion; about Carlos Gardel, whom he considered had taken the tango from its high level of sexuality and Palermo hooliganism to its Paris decadence; about Perón, who was a coward; about the Kabbalah, which saw the universe as a string of verbal symbols uttered by a mathematical God.

Our limo driver was a scrawny red-headed gentleman in a checkered hat and old leather jacket. He *sirred* us and *ma'ammed* us as we entered the car, but then said nothing till we reached our destination.

"Have I ever confessed to you about my having come upon a British title?" Borges said out of the blue.

"No, you haven't, and I'm afraid I will be impressed."

"It was some years ago. The English queen charged her ambassador in Buenos Aires with the task of knighting me."

"Sir Jorge Luis!"

"From now on in our Old English lessons, you must treat me with respect, as one worthy of teaching Old English, as one entitled to teach Old English."

"But how can I think of respecting a man who is merely 'Sir George Louis' when I've been used to thinking of your grandfathers who had real titles, Colonel Suárez and Colonel Borges? Ones they earned on the field, not behind some desk behind the front lines."

"You have unmasked me again, Willis."

"Worse, I've returned you to the romance of your military ancestry. I must warn María not to let you remove those small portraits of your grandfathers from the tables in your apartment and substitute a portrait of Sir George Louis with a proper sash or garter. I admit you would look jolly in a garter."

"Jolly Englishman I am not, but I have also confessed to being partial to the English translation of *Don Quijote* over the barbaric original."

"I've read *Pierre Menard.*"

"And if I could read Arabic," he declared, "I'd still prefer Richard Burton's loving prodigality to the legendary stylistic poverty of the original *Nights.*"

"Even though he was an obscene Victorian who wrote about his personal experiences in a Bengal brothel?"

"I'll have to reconsider the translation by Sir Richard."

We reached southern Indiana near midnight. After we pulled up to the Indiana University Memorial Union, where Borges and María were staying, the silent driver leaped out, opened our door. The 1980 election campaign was taking place in all its unnatural fury. Our driver seemed to look up at Borges, although he was actually taller than Borges. Drawing himself very erect he said to him, stuttering but with strong emotion: "Sir, I don't know what your n-n-name is or who you are. But would you consider running for president? We stand in n-n-need of you." It was a request, but he was adamant.

Again Seneca had spoken.

Failed Vision in Cambridge

"I am looking at beautiful images. You have given me an exhibition of something graphic which I find exhilarating. I see clouds. I see red moons, black moons, circling in the greenish mist. They are not letters, however. Is there really a page under this machine, or is this a silent picture of the skies of Paradise?"

Back in New York we were in a taxi again, crossing the Brooklyn Bridge. It was midnight, and we had just returned from Cambridge. I had gone alone with Borges; María had stayed in New York. It was his first trip there in years, to that city where in 1968 he was in residence as the Charles Eliot Norton lecturer at Harvard. Borges was nostalgic and spoke of Cambridge as a favorite residence of the past, comparing it with Geneva; he evoked doubles of other Borgeses who lived in those cities, of younger and older Borgeses who talked to each other on park benches in front of the Charles, on the shore of Lac Léman, in the cafés of both cities. Borges made real the discrete periods of time by recalling and inventing characters bearing his name to converse with each other.

Yet, for all his enthusiasm, something had made him wish either to skip the trip, or at least to arrive late. In the end he always went to every destination planned, but not without protest.

Earlier in the afternoon we had been about to take the shuttle to Boston. You buy the tickets on the plane. As we neared the plane, Borges slowed. Since it left on the hour, he decided that while he would like to have time to walk around Cambridge, still he wanted to stand there on the field and *charlar* about the Cambridge we were going to. He spoke about Juan Marichal, the Spanish historian at Harvard, and his wife, Solita, the daughter of the Spanish poet Pedro Salinas. Juan was his friend, caring and conscientious almost to a fault. Juan would be waiting for us at MIT, where the chat was to take place. But Borges was more eager to talk about seeing Marichal again than he was to be in Cambridge with him.

"A very intense man," he said. "I've been told he looks like an

English king, with the serious profile you find on British stamps. But of course Marichal is more refined and intelligent than those pedestrian English monarchs, those movie stars of sentimental films. It is a tragedy and a mystery about his son Miguel. Juan alluded to it several times but said no more. I've known literary suicides in Argentina. Yes, the old writers do it when they are sick or angry, and then there are the momentarily despairing youths. But why on earth did Miguel kill himself? It is strange to me."

"It is strange. It has encircled me sometimes, but I'm not a candidate."

"Well, I am not afraid of suicide, and certainly not attracted to it, except when Bioy Casares and I talk and do our verbal games. And then it is the concept, not the act. One evening, in a good mood, we asked ourselves should we try it to see what happens? The next morning, when I woke, I had to think very carefully whether I'd done so. But Miguel. Why on earth? . . ."

"I don't know, Borges, but I remember so many years ago when Solita was pregnant with Miguel. It was 1947. I spent a week visiting her brother Jaime (who had just dropped out of college) at Pedro Salinas's house in Baltimore. Although the Spanish poet had been in this country more than a decade, he spoke little English. But those evenings, hearing him speak about Spanish poets and poetry, turned me to the Spanish poets. One late afternoon Solita showed up at the door. I remember her face then as vividly as I see yours now beside me. It is terrible to think of someone you remember as a pleasant protrusion in his mother's belly, who later is a handsome graduate student finishing a doctorate in linguistics at Stanford, who then throws himself off a California freeway crossover bridge down into the oncoming traffic. I went to the cemetery in Cambridge with Juan one afternoon. A cemetery more like an old private New England estate. It was a lovely day, of great serenity, and the cemetery, more a garden than a graveyard, had the heavy aroma of flowers and the intensity of the rhododendrons. Miguel's death put Juan in the hospital. I was young when my father threw himself off a rooftop in Colorado, but I have never been able to bury my father. He comes back regularly in dreams, even last year in China, and we meet secretly, and happily, someplace where no one knows us."

"Barnstone, you are making me miss the plane. I must thank you for that and for talking so much."

"You are too polite, as they say in Chinese. And worse, you are teaching me bad lessons. Supposing I turned out to be like you?"

"You'd have my sincere condolences."

"As for why Miguel did it, can anyone know? Did Miguel himself know? I remember him as a person of quiet poise and unusual wisdom and dignity for one so young. A beauty about him. But who has seen those demons? Commonly it's manic depression, a change in medicines, or something idiotic happening just before the action. Trivial, of course, but irreversible."

"Lugones killed himself, but his motive was revenge. He was a remarkable writer. All of us revered and rejected him, imitated and decried him. Lugones killed himself because he wanted to kill or wound a friend."

"Borges, you are the least suicidal person I've known. Even though you may beef about being Borges, of living on in this world which is often a wearisome darkness. I'll bet on you till the last breath."

"Your money is safe."

"We can get the five o'clock plane. We'll just have less time in Cambridge."

Borges liked to play with authority. He never did what he was supposed to as a writer, as a citizen. His loyalty was to family and friends; for the rest, he was the heresiarch of his Syrian or Alexandrian Gnostics. He liked the history of infamy, the history of the art of verbal abuse that no one could practice like Swift, Voltaire, Shaw, or Quevedo. He liked the form of insulting people that the dog permits—"O dog of the desert," a denunciation recorded in the 146th Night of *A Thousand and One Nights,* or to dip into "an alphabet of scorn." His serious disdain for authority is contemptuously displayed in a popular tale he picked up in Geneva, when he lived there as a young man late in World War I: "Miguel Servet's reply to the judges who had condemned him to the stake: 'I will burn, but this is a mere event. We shall continue our discussion in eternity' " (*Borges, a Reader,* 49).

His opposition to contemporary public authority coincided with his literary idiolect, his very personal canon of major writers, and, in friendship and marriage, to a dependence, because of blindness, on others, together with a fierce resentment of all confining help. Those of us who remained his friends for many years were aware of his ultimate exasperation with those who were too helpful, too readily his benefactors. In his mind there was a nervous line of discretion between liberation and imprisonment. When he felt imprisoned, he freed himself.

One of Borges's old friends, who helped him, perhaps more than anyone, to become internationally known, through English translation and lucrative contracts, was Norman Thomas di Giovanni. The story of their friendship, collaboration, and final dissolution of all ties reflects the antinomical Borges, exemplifies the conflict between dependence and freedom.

My life was early connected with Norman, or Digi, as he called himself then. I was a graduate student at Yale, living in West Haven in a cold cottage, with a badly fitting stained-glass church panel as the front wall against the colds of New Haven Sound. One day in 1956 my friend Mark Strand, then a painter in the School of Art and Architecture, brought his student friend from Antioch College for a visit. Once he learned that in Spain I had done a booklength translation of the poems of the Spanish poet Antonio Machado, di Giovanni immediately took charge of me. He offered to edit it, bullied me into using rhyme, fought with me through the proofs about words, especially about *and* and *the,* which he was not fond of in those days. He moved in for a few weeks so as not to waste time and to keep tabs on me. I am grateful for his bullying and his editing skills. There were many adventures. Later, when I was editing *Hispanic Arts* \ *Artes Hispanicas* for Macmillan, I asked him to guest edit a number dedicated to Borges's poems. He completed the manuscript for me, and we got as far as page proof for that number before the journal folded for lack of funds. That issue of Borges's poems, intact, soon afterward became his Delacorte *Selected Poems* of Borges.

On another occasion, in 1967, Juan Marichal asked me to arrange a poetry reading for Borges in English and Spanish at the Poetry Center at the New York Y. Di Giovanni heard about the reading and wrote, offering to be of local help. It took place the following spring — a memorable reading, each poem followed by Borges's comments. Soon after, Norman was in Argentina with Borges. For three years they worked like demons — or I should say di Giovanni worked with Borges, developing their distinctive translations of the stories, poems, and such volumes as *The Book of Imaginary Beings.* Di Giovanni obtained an attractive first refusal contract from *The New Yorker,* took care of rights, obtained respectable royalties for himself for the English translations. He was Borges's secretary for letters and dictation, his boss as well. He got Borges to prepare the unique long autobiographical essay that appears as an afterword to *The Aleph and Other Stories, 1933–1969* (1970). He traveled with Borges. He was like a brother, uncle, son, and when Borges married his childhood sweetheart after a forty-year wait, di Giovanni was there as a rival, helping Borges to dissolve this unhappy marriage. He was also a rival to Borges's other mate: his mother, Leonor. All this is straightforward and public. And then around 1972 they parted, in effect forever, though there was one momentary meeting in Chicago in 1982.

I have gone into some detail to speak of this collaboration and friendship, since it shows a pattern. Why did the valuable relationship fall apart? It was not simply Norman's personality. Borges often talked to me about Norman. I listened with a certain reluctance. Borges would say to me, "You are a poet, Barnstone; di Giovanni simply translated my poems." I took this not as a compliment to myself but as an expression of displeasure with di Giovanni, as well as an unfair judgment, since his prose and poetry translations are uniformly remarkable. I knew that Borges's strongest feelings were of lingering resentment against di Giovanni. Why? They had translated together for three years, rewritten the English, even gone back at times and retouched the Spanish as a result of the English translation.

In more cheerful commentaries Borges would tell me—and he often repeated his wondrous stories—how he called Norman "Nap."

"Nap?" I said.

"Yes, Nap. For Napoleon. He was short, he took charge like a general and gave me orders, which I sometimes listened to. It was his manner and method. Did I tell you how we parted company?"

The first time Borges related this story was at the entrance to his house, as we were about to go on an evening walk. Then, at the corner of Paraguay and Córdoba in the Saint James Café, under the double mirrors where Borges and his others shone, he repeated the episode in the very same words.

"In the period when I was trying to find myself after my disastrous marriage, di Giovanni called me one afternoon to let me know that he had used some of my funds to make a deposit on an apartment in which we could all live together. That evening—it was a Sunday—at Bioy Casares's house, I said to myself enough is enough. We were eating dinner and between the soup and the main course I got up,

went to the phone and called him. I said only three words to him:
'Norman, we're through.' Then I hung up. I did not see him again.
It only took the time between the soup and the main course. Then
I went back to the table and told Adolfo that I had broken with di
Giovanni."

"You mean . . ."

"The time between the soup and the main course," he repeated,
sternly. He was chuckling.

The reason for their split involed Borges's survival. He was helped,
let us say nurtured in his international reputation, by the enterprising
and endlessly energetic Norman Thomas di Giovanni. But in the end
Borges knew he was in prison. The pattern was repeated, with variations, with other devotees. There were always specific pretexts, but
the rupture was due to Borges's need to free himself from so much
service, dependence, management.

Borges had only one father, one mother, and they could not be
replaced, at least not permanently. Emir Rodríguez Monegal argues
eloquently that patricide, though repressed, runs through Borges's
work and his posture to the past; moreoever, that Borges had an ironic
need for and indulgence in immediate literary patricide. While Monegal is keen in his analysis of Borges's need to be free from his
father, as well as from all who have helped him too much, personally
I heard only unrepressed praise, even reverence, from Borges's lips.
He expressed sympathy for his father's blindness, praise for his counsel
and wisdom—frequently. Whatever Oedipal weapons may have been
lurking in the inner labyrinth, such knives never floated into the
daylight. His public posture gave one clear sign: his father was the
one nonmilitary male ancestor he spoke about and the sole ancestor
he wished to emulate. Borges often said, with filial loyalty, that he
intended to finish and publish his father's unfinished novel. He didn't
finish it; nor did he ever write his projected books on Silesius and
Swedenborg. This in no way diminished his loyalty to these heroes.
And wherever he might be, in the streets of his city, walking through
a lost neighborhood in the evening rain, his father returned to him:

Rain

Suddenly the afternoon is clear and wan
with light, for now a minute rain is falling.
Falling and fell. The drizzle is a thing

That takes place surely in a past that's gone.
Whoever hears it falling is refed
With time in which mere chance begins to feel
A flower whose name is *rose,* and to reveal
The curious pigment of the color red.
This shower, darkening blind the windowpane,
Will brighten some lost neighborhoods with rain
On black grapes and an arbor that divide
A backyard that is gone forever. Moist
Evening brings back the voice, the wanted voice:
My father coming back, who hasn't died.

Even with a lifetime of read books in his memory, research and wide reading were not easy in these last years. He once said to me, with the pleasure of resignation, "I do mostly the shorter forms now, poems and stories, but not essays, since they require a kind of reading that is now too difficult for me." Yet Borges continued to brush up older essays, editing and expanding them. He issued books of his lectures on Dante and continued writing his unique introductions, including even an introduction to a book of his introductions.

Being interested in memory, Borges often quoted his father's advice for retaining an accurate memory of an event: Don't recall a memory back into consciousness, for in doing so the memory is changed. The next recollection will contain not only the first memory but also the second memory of a memory of the event, and so on, until the orginal is lost. Borges was also loyal to his living family members, except at the very end, where again there was a threat to his desire for another kind of freedom: the freedom to choose and commit himself to his last companion, to resolve his decades of friendship with María Kodama via his deathbed marriage. It was the consummation of Borges's life near his death, and, in my opinion, his most noble, moral, and romantic act.

Totally opposed by his Argentine family, legally opposed, financially opposed, Borges reacted as he had toward earlier benefactors. But now the antagonists were his sister, his nephews, and Fanny, his servant, who was the same as family. In the conflict between dependence and freedom, he decisively chose freedom, which he made clear in his acts, his will, his public statements. Borges was again *free,* and died. I cannot help recalling the words that Nikos Kazantzakis had inscribed in a cliffside in Crete, chosen as the tomb for his ashes: *Den thelo típote. Den fováme típote. Eimei eléftheros.* (I want nothing, I fear nothing. I am free.) The last external authorities were overcome. Going into pleasant exile in Geneva (since divorce and remarriage were illegal in Catholic Argentina), Borges acted freely, outwitting authority, and chose his own posture before death.

Norman Thomas di Giovanni reentered the picture in a detective story of three continents. The episode began at the University of Texas, a favorite haunt of Borges. In 1961 he had there spent his first semester at an American university. The late Miguel Enguídanos took a striking photo of Borges and his mother at the Alamo, posing handsome, stylish and smiling like a couple who had just emerged from a Ferrari to stand before the rusty stone of the old ruin. In the summer of 1977 I was teaching in Austin. My boss was Michael Holquist, then chair of comparative literature, who became one of my most beloved friends. One day Holquist took me aside to tell me something very confidential.

"I think you were a friend of di Giovanni."

"What's up, Mike?"

"He was killed in a car accident in Scotland."

I was stunned with sadness, including the sadness of incompletion that death signifies, battering one with remorse.

"Where did you get that information?"

"I can't tell you."

"I don't understand."

"I'm sorry, Willis."

A week or so later we spoke about it again. Holquist was more relaxed but still strangely evasive. "The information came from an Argentine professor of history. And it's absolutely authentic."

"Where'd he hear it?"

"From Borges."

"I'll write Borges."

I kept the knowledge of Norman's death with me for the next year. Nap was gone. It seemed like a short time ago that he had shown up in West Haven, moved in with me and put me to work on Machado. One day, out of thin air, he had announced defiantly, "Yeah, Willis, who knows, some time or other I might get screwed into marriage, but I'll never have any brats."

He was soon to marry Priscilla — I remember an uproarious shower the couple took together in his Boston hangout. Digi had the energy of a bull. Later he was to break the vow on having brats.

"Why not have kids?" I said incredulously. "I thought you were crazy about Aliki."

My daughter Aliki was crawling, beautiful on the very cold early spring floor.

"Aliki doesn't count," he snarled. "She's one in a million, she doesn't count."

I relished his harsh affection for her.

Memories of Digi, the son of an anarchist Italian-American gardener from Boston, who had given him the socialist name Norman Thomas.

Then, to my puzzlement, about a year after leaving Texas, I read that di Giovanni was publishing a new translation of Borges. I assumed it was a posthumous translation from the backlog of their years together. But no, it was a very live di Giovanni who was publishing the new volume.

Eventually I discovered the key.

Meanwhile, Borges was informed that Norman was alive, and he was relieved. He had been very upset upon receiving the news of his death. As the curious hints from Scotland, Austin, and Buenos Aires were sorted out, the mists surrounding Norman's disappearance and resurrection dissolved. Apparently, in a casual conversation with a gentleman from Austin, Borges had said flippantly that he hadn't heard a word from di Giovanni in years; for all he knew, he might have been killed in an automobile accident in Scotland.

The word spread. Borges, the Funes of memory, had no recollection of his offhand quip when news of Norman's death came back to him dramatically. Paul reappeared after his historical execution in a Roman cell to write his last epistles (if we are to believe their ascription to him), and both Mark Twain and Ernest Hemingway had the opportunity to read obituaries written for their misreported deaths — "Reports of my death have been greatly exaggerated," Twain noted. Borges, aided by others' misinterpretation and his own small lapse of memory, had invented the violent death of his old companion Norman Thomas di Giovanni.

We stepped into the five o'clock plane to Boston, reached the city of Puritans and great academies, and quickly found ourselves in an

MIT dining room. Juan and Solita were there, as were Stephen Gill-
man, a professor of Spanish at Harvard and son-in-law of the Spanish
poet Jorge Guillén, and a few others. As I greeted Stephen, whom I
had not seen in years, he smiled and accusingly asked whether I was
now doing the di Giovanni act of taking Borges around for lectures.
I mumbled something back. Apart from feeling a little abused, I felt
for María. As she frequently complained to me, she had to suffer
almost daily putdowns when people who wished to speak to Borges
typed her as the intermediary who was to be flattered or scorned, but
not to be seen naturally, as a person herself.

Borges's talk went well, as always. After the formal talk, as soon
as we turned off the mikes, there was mayhem — no María to thread
us through the labyrinth. Borges seemed especially pleased with the
pandemonium, during which he was handshaking and scribbling his
secret Chinese character seal on books owned by unseen faces. He
especially liked exchanging thoughts with his friend Jaime Alazraki,
who had Borges take him by the arm and go with him to the room
of a student who had a special optical instrument that might be
helpful to Borges. Jaime, then teaching at Harvard, had studied Kabbalah in Jerusalem with Gershom Scholem, one of Borges's favorite
sources of Jewish mysticism.

I had agreed to take Borges to the room of an MIT Korean graduate
student, where we would try out his device for enlarging page print.
We had very high hopes, at least I did. And I still had pangs about
a recent disappointment in Bloomington, when the medical inventors
of eye prisms who held out promise of improved vision ended up
doing nothing for his eyes. I had hoped that, through some disguised
conspiracy between science and Borges, a sensible miracle could be
worked out. The last step on the way to failure took place that evening
in Cambridge.

The trip across campus was unusually hurried, since we did want
to catch a midnight plane back to New York. All of Cambridge and
Boston, it seemed, was there to greet Borges, to walk with him. By
the time we reached Kim Lo's room, ten minutes and many dingy
corridors away, we were many dozens. I managed politely to leave
the group outside the door while Borges sat down before the machine.
We were suddenly alone, and the noise of near silence was overwhelming. It was the loud silence between notes. I wish Borges could
have imitated the Spanish mystic John of the Cross, who heard *la*

musica callada (the music of a silence), climbed the mountain of vision, and there, by lion caves, looked out to see light everywhere.

Borges's vision was to remain interior, like his dream landscapes. With great care Kim put the machine over a book and fitted Borges's face into the special lenses that compensated for Kim's own detached retinas.

Borges's first reaction was a tremendous smile. He said he saw wonderful things. He claimed to be very happy with what he saw. He was now on Patmos, had climbed away from his stone pillow in the cave of the Apocalypse, had climbed the ramparts of the Byzantine monastery of Ayos Jannis, and described the panorama. Actually, he was the Castilian barber Sancho, mounted on his rockinghorse Clavileño, Sancho Panza the joyful actor reading aloud the wayward fantasy of his cunning mind.

"I am looking at beautiful images. You have given me an exhibition of something graphic which I find exhilarating. I see clouds. I see red moons, black moons, circling in the greenish mist. They are not letters, however. Is there really a page under this machine, or is this a silent movie of the skies of Paradise?"

Borges's eyes began to fail dramatically in his mid-fifties. He managed well, wrote about blindness and found himself switching identities, as in *The Maker,* from blind Homer to Milton, who reached for his late wife only to find — as did Aeneas in Hades, when he moved to embrace his father — only shadow. But shadow and its praise, *Elogio de la sombra* (In Praise of Shadow), became a center of his experience in poetry. In his last book, *Los conjurados* (The Conspirators), he included the poem "On his blindness," whose title (except for the lower caps) is from Milton's famous sonnet bearing the same title:

> After these many years, circling near
> me is an obstinate and luminous haze
> reducing things to just one thing: a maze
> formless and colorless, almost a mere
> idea. Vast elemental night and day,
> swarming with people, are that blur of light,
> dubious, faithful, never dropping away,
> that lies in wait at dawn. I would like sight

to see a face at last. I can't know old
and unexplored encyclopedias, the prize
of books that just my hand can recognize,
birds in the firmament and moons of gold.
For others there remains the universe;
in my half-light: the habit of my verse.

For all the compensations, to be blind was not desirable for Borges, as it is not for anyone. Except for those last few months in Italy and Switzerland, when his health was failing but his company constant, the blindness also reflected the darkness of his increasing sense of loneliness, the loneliness of the habitual insomniac. Borges told me his eyes were improving. His doctor was giving him vitamin shots in the bottom and warned him not to let others experiment with his eyes. In 1980, when we were in America at the same time, I called Boston and managed to get him an appointment at the prestigious Boston Eye and Ear Clinic. I called him in Washington, reaching him in the evening at his hotel.

"Look here, Willis, I'm very nervous."

Indeed, he was agitated. I could hear it in his voice. I realized, then, that here on the phone we were both blind men, and with Borges having a certain advantage of experience. Blindness—or its absence—is also a habit of thought.

"What in the world happened?" I asked.

"You know some of my best friends are journalists. There is Monegal, there is. . . ."

"And so," I interrupted.

"And there are others who ask me questions, who overhear me, whom I can't see and don't know are journalists, who quote me, and all the time I have confused them with human beings."

"What happened today?"

"I was at some official event in Washington and a journalist came to me. Seeing that I was Argentine and since he knew about the musical *Evita*, he put two and two together and asked me what I thought of the real Evita. I mean, not about the musical but *la puta* (the whore). Yes, when they asked me about Evita, I said she was a *puta*. As soon as I said it I bit my tongue, because I knew it would be in all the papers. But in fact she was a whore, and I am not speaking figuratively, but accurately, about her worthy profession before Juan Perón transformed her into a popular Argentine saint."

"I bet the papers won't pick up on it."

"I couldn't help it," he went on. "The words came out of my mouth before I knew it. Of course you know that Juan Perón tried once to rename our beautiful city of La Plata after Evita, and the only name he could come up with was *La Pluta.*"

"Borges, I'm trying to get you to an eye doctor and you're cracking jokes about Evita the whore."

"We can look into it in Bloomington," he compromised.

This was a victory! Initially he had been unwilling to make any move in this direction.

"Why do you resist so much?" I asked him one day.

"Because I'm a coward. I don't like physical pain. Ask my dentist."

In Indiana, a few weeks later, on their second stay in Bloomington, where this time Borges and María remained a month, I did manage to arrange an appointment for Borges. He was to see a pioneer doctor who designed glasses for people who had virtually no vision. The doctor had the reputation of making the blind see.

During the preliminary examination Borges was jumpy. What made things worse was that the intern who began the examination, and who spoke in a heavy dialect of Southern Indiana, assumed that Borges was someone he could not understand and asked me to interpret his remarks. Borges speaks impeccable English, albeit, as he asserts, a bit nineteenth-centuryish. He was more disturbed than amused. Had it been another occasion, he would have laughed at all the ironies, and even brought in Zeno's paradox of the tortoise. But given his uneasiness, he said to María, "Shall we go?"

"No," María calmly replied.

María's assurance was enough. The pioneer doctor didn't show up. A second doctor, however, overseeing the intern, did come in with hurried authority and described Borges's problem as detached retinas. There was no possibility of restoring his sight through a laser operation, but he suggested that Borges might very much improve his vision through special lenses. We made an appointment for the following week to see the elusive expert who would design such glasses.

Scheduling problems and distracting events prevented us from keeping that appointment. I held myself responsible and felt terrible. Borges was pleased by our missed appointment, like a schoolboy who got off the hook, scot-free. I told him so, with just those words. Borges didn't criticize my mixed metaphors, but got away from his eyes and went off into his love for Scottish speech.

"Look here, the Scots haven't let the early centuries slip away from them. The Scotch-speaking ones hang onto the old Germanic sounds, perhaps with the helpful memory of when they were speaking Celtic. I heard them in Edinburgh. With their rolling rs and resonating consonants, a good Scot sounds closer to how Shakespeare spoke than does any actor on the London stage. And when a learned Scot takes to reading Old English aloud, it's dessert and glory."

At least one very happy event did occur in Bloomington, testing and proving the worth of Borges's vision, even if it was through Plato's third eye of the imagination—or, more appropriately, the mythical eye of Cyclops. On a late afternoon Borges and María came for tea in the barn house where my wife, Helle Phaedra, and I lived. That day he saw everything. As they walked down the stairs, under the long Saxon sleepers that characterize old Hoosier barn joinery, Borges said, "I feel I'm on a ship. There is so much wood around me."

We sat at a marble table. I told them I had bought the table a few years earlier in New York. The store owner said it was Spanish marble. I asked him what part of Spain, and he said, "Portugal."

"I'm like the marble. I am Borges from Spain, from the grape and cork province of Portugal."

Helle was born in Príngipos, on Prince Island in the Golden Horn, a few hours from Constantinople. She was Helle for being born near the Hellespont, the Sea of Helle, where her namesake had fallen off the slippery back of the Golden Fleece into the sea while she and her brother Frixos were fleeing Zeus's usually jealous consort. Borges asked Helle many questions about Greece, and then complained about his experience in Athens.

"I was in Athens for just a few days, but the Argentine ambassador got hold of me and wouldn't let me out of his claws. I didn't climb the Acropolis, mind you. I did not get to see the Parthenon."

"Borges!"

I remembered my first climb up to the marble city. It was 1949. The civil war, except in parts of Crete and near Albania, was over. I went with the English poet Louis MacNeice, who had just come to Greece to head the British Institute. After a hundred meters MacNeice, a tall, dark, handsome Irishman, stumbled in the rubble and fell to the ground. He hit his head on a fragment of marble, got up, wiped the blood off his temple with a handkerchief, looked at it and was very pleased, on that first day, to have mixed his blood with the stone of the Acropolis.

"Did you hear much Greek music, the *rembetika?* The popular dancing of the taverns?" Helle said. "It's from the region where I was born. Constantipole, Smyrna, Asia Minor."

"*Rembetika* is something like the old tango danced by *compadritos* in the bordellos," I said. "There's the young hero, the *palikari* or *mangas,* but the words in these tavern songs of the poor worker, though sometimes expressing clever bravado, have more pathos, are more elemental and tragic. And the melody doesn't come to a climax as in European music. It goes on, it persists indefinitely."

Helle put on a record. Tsitsanis. Heavy *rembetika,* the *cante jondo* of Greek popular song. We danced. Helle is a superb dancer. Through his blind eyes Borges saw everything. The music, Tsistanis's bouzouki, were intoxicating, and María kept saying, "We never saw or heard this in Greece." She joined us for a while in the *hassapiko,* the dance of the Byzantine butchers' guild. Borges's relaxed gaze was full of mischievous pleasure. The poet always confessed that music (except for a little Brahms) was his weakest art, but that afternoon for an hour he watched us clearly and heard the *rembetika* songs. The words sounded like an ancient indecipherable but familiar Spanish, and his observing eyes looked like he was drunk.

Years later, in Geneva, in one of his last prose poems, he evokes an overheard music drifting down from a hilltop: "This night, not far from the summit of Saint Pierre, a wondrous Greek music full of venture has just revealed to us that death is more unbelievable than life and that, therefore, the soul persists when the body is chaos" (*Los conjurados,* 35).

Borges's observing eyes. As for improving his sight, he gave the impression of unconcern, though he was enthusiastic whenever he could make out an object that he thought was previously denied him. I can't say why I had become so concerned, even guilty about his loss of sight. After all, the vision of the blindman was central to the deepening personalization and pathos of his last books. In the poems the shift is clear, from the sighted to the blind observer. Among other aspects of his altered vision is the large number of humane portraits

of other poetic figures—Heine, Whitman, Keats, Browning, Spinoza—
where his interest is focused on the person as a writer, and with
crystal compassion.

After many promising hints and hopes of improvement I was
dejected about his Washington refusal to see a Boston specialist, and
the letdowns in Bloomington and Cambridge. But then other thoughts
about Borges, his wit and humanity took over and I saw things with
more balance. I could not help thinking back to what some might
consider a humiliating experience, although I did not. It had occurred
a few years earlier at the domestic airport in Buenos Aires, while we
were waiting for the delayed plane that was to take us to Córdoba.
Borges had to go to the men's room. I had once seen him walk alone
into the women's room at an airport. A young woman, smiling,
kindly walked him back out and led him to the right door. In the
men's room, perhaps to distract from the earthly purposes of the visit,
he was always at his conversational best.

"Barnstone, do you know why Heine liked to receive German
guests in his flat in Paris during the last years of his life, when he
was confined to his so-called death-mattress?"

"Honestly, I don't know. Maybe he missed the good old smells of
German cooking, and wanted to chat about sausages and kings?"

"Now, you know that Heine went through humiliating episodes
due to his having been born a Jew, to his being a Jew. Like other
prominent nineteenth-century Jews, he went through a sham con-
version. It happened to Disraeli, and something of that order to Marx
and Mendelssohn. And remember that Mendelssohn was the grandson
of that famous rabbi in Schiller's play, *Nathan the Wise.*"

"So why did he want to see German tourists?"

With a twinkle he retorted, "So he would keep remembering why
he had absolutely no desire to return to Germany."

Borges often said that his poets in Geneva as a very young man
were Walt Whitman and Heinrich Heine, the latter embodying for
him the German language. In his lingering sickness in exile from
Germany, Heine's posture was stoic in the face of a death from which
even the nightingales of his poetry would not save him:

Paris, 1856

The long prostration has accustomed him
To anticipate his death. His concrete dread

Is going out of doors into the whim
Of day to walk about with friends. Ravaged,
Heinrich Heine thinks about that river
Of time that slowly moves away into
That lingering penumbra and the bitter
Hurt destiny of being a man and Jew.
He thinks about exquisite melodies
Whose instrument he was, and yet he knows
The trilling doesn't come from trees or birds
But time and from the days' slim vagaries.
And yet his nightingales won't save him, no,
Nor nights of gold, nor flowers of sung words.

Borges was in love with the German language—he has a fine poem on the German language—and with its poets and philosophers. When he appeared in Germany he was popular to the point of being a cult hero. He claimed he liked German literature and gave up on the French writers, especially Baudelaire.

I was always irritated when he spoke of his dislike for French or Spanish writers (the latter being even less true, beginning with his hero, Cervantes), though I could never know for sure about any such opinons. After all, Borges accompanied ridicule of Baudelaire with sonorous recitals of his important poems; each verse sounded magnificent, given Borges's special voice for the rhythm and his somber incantation.

But in matters of Jew versus German, Borges had his preference. He would say that the Germans did very well writing in their special Germanic dialect of Yiddish, the richer and more colorful master tongue. Kafka was the model for his fantastic fiction, as was Whitman for the energy of his far-ranging, cataloging poetry. With eloquence, wisdom, and measure, his genial essay "Kafka and His Precursors" anticipates intertextuality, misreading, and reader-response theory. It might have been rewritten as "Borges and His Precursors," in which Kafka is Borges's literary creation.

So there we were, both standing next to the urinals, discussing Heine (whom he had learned to read with a dictionary in his late teens in Geneva as his means of learning to read German), the German language itself, and Kafka. When Borges finished his duty standing at the tiled wall, I noticed that his shoes were covered with urine.

Borges remarked, "You know, now I can make out some of those squares. I couldn't do it a few years ago."

He fingered the lines of the tiles, putting his face very near the wall over the urinal.

"I can decipher the color."

"What color is it?"

"Yellow, I think. Yes, it is yellow."

I could not let the poet walk out of there with his feet wet with piss.

"Borges, excuse me, you got your shoes covered with mud. You always had a secret double who was a hippie bohemian." I took some paper towels and dried his shoes.

"You know, I like to walk in the slums. I can breathe when I walk in the slums."

As Borges talked about the slum barrios, I recalled his early piece about Palmero, Buenos Aires, from his biography of Evaristo Carriego. It ends with his description of the rough, largely Italian barrio of his childhood: "For Buenos Aires is unfathomably deep, and I have never given myself over to its streets without receiving, however great my disillusionment or anguish, unexpected consolation — now a sense of unreality, now a guitar in a hidden patio, now a brush with other lives. 'Here and here did England help me' [said Browning]— here and here did Buenos Aires come to help me" (*Borges, a Reader,* 22).

Although Borges accepted his condition of darkness with no hope of radical change, still he liked to clown about his vision, as about so many things. One evening, in a rundown small auditorium in Buenos Aires where he was to give a talk, he complained, strangely, that he couldn't see very well.

"Well, if you can't see, try my glasses," I suggested.

"I handed him my gold wire-rims, which he slipped on for the rest of the evening. He gave his talk and later signed books while wearing them. A photograph with those glasses is frequently reproduced. That evening, at a supper, Borges tried on everybody's glasses at the table, one by one. And one by one he declared their virtues and defects and described his own extravagant visions granted him by each pair. He did not often miss a chance to have fun.

As we returned home in a long car ride through the barrios of Buenos Aires, for a while I watched the summer night of December, usually filled with passersby, even at this late hour, but now almost deserted because of a sudden rainstorm. The city skirmishes between police and *Montoneros* was, I thought, probably on hold because of bad weather. There is something haunting about gazing through city rain, after midnight, while in a car speeding through the disappearing streets.

"Borges, what are your thoughts now that this evening you've recovered your vision?"

"My vision. Walt Whitman had a vision, and I have always admired him for it. I mean the one who invented the pen of Walt Whitman. I learned what modern poetry was from him, and his 'Lilacs' for Lincoln are unsurpassed. 'When Lilacs Last in the Dooryard Bloom'd' is—well, it is perhaps the greatest elegy in the English language. As for the failed Whitman, the person who couldn't hold down a job, who was perhaps more unhappy than he was heroic: I care for him also, and feel even closer to him. And I am indebted to him. Perhaps I cannot learn what poetry is from Walter Whitman. Though if I were worthy of this failed Whitman, this literary bungler, I would learn from the weaknesses we share, our insecurities, our transparent gestures revealing our little vanities, which we mask in art. I would learn from this master of common humanity."

I remembered Borges's poem on Whitman. It depicts the old poet, like Borges, filling the mirror with his gaze and declaring his uncertain vision boldly, and so revealing it was Walter, still trying to be Walt:

Camden, 1892

The smell of coffee and of newspapers.
Sunday and its monotony. The morning,
Some allegoric verses are adorning
The glimpsed-at page, the vain pentameters
Of a contented colleague. The old man lies
Stretched out and white in his respectable
Poor man's room. Then lazily he fills
The weary mirror with his gaze. His eyes
See a face. Unsurprised he thinks: That face
Is me. With fumbling hand he reaches out
To touch the tangled beard and ravaged mouth.
The end is not far off. His voice declares:
I'm almost gone and yet my verses scan
Life and its splendor. I was Walt Whitman.

"Well, I guess I asked you about your recovered vision, and you gave me Whitman. Thank you."

"But why not Whitman? I am hardly worthy of that ordinary giant—yet I suppose I am hardly worthy of any of those poets, of those real poets I read and reread. All contemporary literature would be different had America not given the world the works of this lonely man from Brooklyn. But look here, Barnstone, as usual I have strayed. You asked me an essential question, about vision, although of course you were playing with the word *vision*, meaning something quite important and impossible, and at the same time you had in mind my bad eyes. But I have a pat answer for both aspects of your question, and it is short and sweet: I am constantly being baffled by things."

"You could use that metaphysical alibi as an answer to any question."

"I could, and perhaps I should. There is something definitive about bafflement, isn't there? Since it opens the way to knowledge yet precludes arrival. Maybe Baudelaire—the one you like and I find merely great—was perfectly right when he wrote *against* arrival in that wonderful poem about the mystery of loss, 'Chant d'automne': *Ce bruit mysterieux sonne comme un départ.* At this moment, Willis, it strikes me that I have for a very long time been unfair to that deeply suffering poet of the city, for we do share the habit of using eternally banal plain rhymes."

A Glimpse in New York

> "I think you are inventing me, Borges."
> "No, you are inventing *me*, but it is a waste, since although I invented myself, I have already disinvented that person called Borges. It's a relief to be free of him, but unfortunately I often forget, and so here I am again, replaying Borges in Chicago, New York, and Buenos Aires."

Borges was scheduled to give a major lecture on Franz Kafka at the 1983 meeting of the Modern Language Association in New York. He was to have been accompanied from Argentina by Carlos Cortínez, who was in Buenos Aires for a year to work with him, but their relationship had already fallen apart. Instead Alastair Reid introduced him. It was a moving lecture. After reading Borges, our reading of Kafka changes perceptibly — to alter a phrase used by Borges in his commentary.

In his essay "Kafka and His Precursors" Borges observes, "The fact is that each writer *creates* his precursors. His work modifies our conception of the past as it will modify the future." He continues, "The poem 'Fear and Scruples' by Robert Browning is like a prophecy of Kafka's stories, but our reading of Kafka refines and changes our reading of the poem perceptibly" (*Borges, a Reader,* 243). In fact, Kafka more than any other author thoroughly pervaded the style, letter, and spirit of Borges; he was the initial principal model from whom Borges never fully strayed. He translated the writings of "Dr. Franz Kafka," as his parents inscribed on the Prague lawyer's all-to-early erected gravestone. Indeed, Borges translated the first collection of Kafka's work into Spanish in 1938. Emir Rodríguez Monegal points out that Borges published *The Metamorphosis* in Spanish just a few months before he began *Pierre Menard* and three years before *The Garden of Forking Paths* (1941), his first volume of fantastic short stories. Kafka gave Borges the general incentive to change from poetry to the fantastic short story.

Now, following his own formula in "Kafka and His Precursors," in his age of achievement Borges created Kafka, through himself. The lecture was jammed. It was Borges's last appearance in America before a large crowd. After the talk, I went to accompany him. I had not seen him for a few years; I had missed him in Madrid. Now I was walking with him. I held his arm.

"It's Willis."

"Oh, how are you, Barnstone?"

"Where's María?"

"She's heard all my stuff so many times. She is almost as weary of it as I am. She's upstairs in her hotel room, waiting for me to finish my performance. I asked you in Chicago why I was doing this kind of thing. You see, I am still doing it. Do you remember in the car, when you were talking to me and paying no attention to the road? I knew you weren't looking at the road, since all the time you were speaking you were looking directly at me."

"You know me."

"Well, I can't say I know myself, but I believe I have acquired a familiarity with this Greek poet from Indiana."

Uneasily, I confessed, "Friends warn me not to look at people when I'm driving, especially if they're in the back seat. And they yell at me not to look down at poems I place on the seat or balance on the dashboard under the windshield. Yes, it probably was a good thing we didn't crash."

"It would have been some kind of solution."

"You're too metaphysical for your own safety. But, as always, you are saved by another reality."

"The other reality is always on the other side. Soon I'll be on the other side," he said gravely, but with a touch of rhetoric and humor.

"You won't make it anyway. You cannot get there because you have too many of your books here, with hoodwinked readers who won't let them disappear. Those books are heavy and will drag you back. You'll never escape."

"But I personally have been escaping that trash all my life! Trash, well—let us say, exercises. None of these writings, as you know, are in my house, and none reread by me."

"Of course. You have good taste. Why should you stain your bookcase with the writings of an obscure Portuguese Jew hiding out at the bottom of the world? Can you imagine what anyone would think if they came upon a work of Borges standing next to one by Samuel Johnson? I thank you for your discretion."

"You're beginning to talk like me. I'm getting confused, or perhaps disarmed. By the way, how is your whale?" he asked me, with a big smile.

"You mean my rose?"

"Yes, the rose, which I suspect is not in hell but someplace up here, perhaps across the street over there, swaying in a small plot in front of a delicatessen. Or maybe hell is just after the traffic signal, two blocks down to the left."

"I think you are inventing me, Borges."

"No, you are inventing *me*, but it is a waste, since although I invented myself, I have already disinvented that person called Borges. It's a relief to be free of him, but unfortunately I often forget, and so here I am again, replaying Borges in Chicago, New York, and Buenos Aires."

"You are stuck in the figure of a writer who likes to dictate and a venerable graying sage who likes to chat about circles whose center is everywhere. Both respond to the name Borges. Those several Borgeses are undoing the past and perversely modifying the future," I said, sententiously.

"Perversely modifying the future? Barnstone, why are you pulling my leg? You insist on taking me seriously, for which I thank you, but I cannot go along with your wishes. I will leave nothing, I tell you, not even my name."

He uttered the last sentence with strange pleasure, with ambivalence and pride. I didn't believe him, of course, at least not the surface level of the words, yet I understood his perfectly consistent posture. Borges would not be caught with the writer Borges.

He went on, "Perhaps a phrase that I have written, unattached to my name, will somehow enter and remain for a time in the Spanish language."

"I hope you will manage to get at least one good phrase into a future library, like that one of your childhood when you speak of yourself in the paradise of your father's library."

"If I were worthy of my father's library!"

"Who knows, Borges? Maybe some foolish people in the future will be duped by you, will not really know you at all, and somehow you will slip in, an outsider, even for more than a phrase or two."

"Then I should indeed be very ashamed of corrupting my father's fine library."

"To use a good Anglo-Saxon word, one you used recently in describing the act of writing, your modesty makes me retch."

"But why do you always defend me?"

"It's your fault. You provoke it."

"You are wrong, you know. It is your 'curious' taste, I'd wager. You are wrong in defending me, as are the others who are fooled by an appearance of erudition and all my early baroque complexity, which embarrasses me. I would like to go to all those bookstores that carry the stuff, buy whatever copies are on the shelf, and contribute the bulk to some conservation project. I mean, recycling. Yes—recycled, who knows how I'd come out? It could only be an improvement."

"Please save a few poems. Just a few poems."

"To tell you the truth, I yield to the fact that you care for the poems, which as you know my good friends in Argentina don't take seriously in the least and think a waste and a distraction. All in all, I suppose I have to thank you for wanting my insignificant pages to survive. But my father, in his good mind, would not. He was a man of discrimination."

"I give up, Borges."

"You mean I have won you over? You have seen the light? And I am in it, looking very pale, old, and thoroughly transparent."

"Yes, it's true. You're a failure. It's clear from the disillusioned crowd of readers who leave your books unread, who shout insults at you in the streets, by the dim words you yourself pronounce on the soon to vanish work of Jorge Luis Borges."

"Amen. I am redeemed and at peace."

By this time we had reached the end of our last brief walk.

"Is there anything you need, anything I can do before you leave town?" I asked.

"We ought to offer a cock to Asclepius."

"Goodbye, Borges. I am sorry not to see María today. And goodbye to you, and thanks for the lovely tie you gave me when we were last together."

"It was María's choice. Goodbye, Willis."

We embraced.

I was to speak to Borges again the next year by phone from China. But this was the last time I was to see him, to take him by the arm or to feel him take me by the arm, on this planet, whether the place be called hell, a rose, or his own apartment on la Calle de Maipú.

With Borges in
Deep South Mountain

"Of course I want to come to China," Borges said heatedly into the phone. "Do you think I would not want to go
to China? Do you suppose me insane? Do you think I
haven't read the *I Ching* and the *Tao Te Ching* and *The
Dream of the Red Chamber?* Do you think I don't know
Buddhist and Taoist scriptures or Kafka's 'The Great Wall of
China' or the deeds of the Son of Heaven, Shih Huang Ti
the Bookburner? Do you imagine I haven't studied the infinite labyrinth of the Yellow Emperor's palace?"

Our last conversation was from China to Buenos Aires. It
was direct, bookish and complex, with a string of regressive symbols.
I was calling him in his apartment on Maipú Street, speaking from
my rooms at the Friendship Hotel.

First I spoke to Fanny, his Indian servant who had cooked for him,
straightened his tie, and combed his hair for many decades. Borges
was very proud of Fanny's natural wisdom and her poetic version of
natural phenomena. He picked up phrases and insights from cab
drivers, maids, and clerks the way he did from Samuel Johnson and
Oscar Wilde. Although Fanny spoke Guaraní fluently with her children and grandchildren, she never translated from one tongue to
another. For her, translation did not exist, Borges said. There was the
sun and moon in Guaraní and *sol* and *luna* in Spanish, all part of
one extended language.

One day Borges was very excited about Fanny's latest theological
insight. That morning she had asked him whether the Japanese had
invented God.

"What gave you that idea?" Borges said.

"I thought the Japanese might have invented God since I knew
they invented flowers," was her reply.

With me, Fanny was always intimate, as if I were one of Borges's
nephews. China was not Japan, but I said to her, "This is Willis, I'm
in China. China. That's right. Yes, China. Is Borges in?"

After a big greeting and talk about Borges's health, diet, and sleeping habits, she said, "You must be very far away. I will get him before we lose you." She put him on the phone.

"*Hola,*" Borges said, his resonating voice rising characteristically into a question.

"Borges, this is Willis. I'm calling from China."

I always called myself Willis, but Borges usually addressed me and all friends by our last names, as he expected us to call him simply Borges. "Not Señor Borges—that is stuffy and sounds very English, like *Mr.* Borges," he would say. In speaking to others about me, however, even in my presence, he switched to my first name. It was a very curious sign of affection, clear in his voice; but of course when we addressed each other man to man it had to be Borges and Barnstone. His last words to me in New York had been "Goodbye, Willis."

Borges was fascinated by etymology and by names. Jorge Luis Borges was an impossible name, he claimed, one he could hardly pronounce himself, and he would intone his own name derisively: "Jorge Luis Borges." In Spanish, he pointed out, the only word that rhymed with Borges was *forges,* the second person subjunctive of *forjar,* to forge.

"No," I told him once, "your own name contains a hidden assonant rhyme in Jorge and Borges. And if we add your Jorge, together with your double, the other Jorge, we have two Jorges, a perfect rhyme: Jorges and Borges. Or best, take you to Cuba or Andalusia where they swallow the final *s* and again the rhyme is perfect: Jorge Lui Borge. But I think your name is impossible because it sounds like a short bad poem."

"My name is pure doggerel, wouldn't you say?" he chortled, with contagious laughter that started low and rose emphatically into a strong epiphany of self-derision.

We had many discussions about rhyme. Late one afternoon, adopting a mock rhetorical voice, he said he was going to let me in on a secret: "When I am restless, searching for a rhyme for a poem, I often wander into the bathroom. As I stand there, shaking the bishop's hand, musing, the rhyme usually comes. Odd, isn't it?"

The Chinese operator interrupted briefly to check on the connection.

"This is Willis," I repeated.

"Barnstone, *A Rose in Hell,*" he said in recognition.

Borges liked to add epithets to people's names. So it was inevitably Heraclitus the Obscure, Spinoza the Lens Grinder, Ezra Pound the Fraud, T. S. Eliot the Good Poet and Stuffy Critic, Robert Frost the Fine Poet and Terrible Farmer, William Butler Yeats the Baroque Gong-Tormented Sea. I was happy about my "Rose in Hell" epithet, since it had a complicated literary genesis.

In 1977 I was reading new poems by Borges. In one sonnet I found the phrase *angel en el infierno* (angel in hell). It gave me the idea for a sonnet, "A Rose in Hell," which I sent to him in Buenos Aires from Indiana, saying I had lifted the title from his sonnet. A week later I called him, and with characteristic flattery and self-deprecation he told me not to worry about the borrowing, since anyway "a rose in hell" was better than "an angel in hell," his worn phrase for Lucifer. Moreover, he said, my "rose" had given *him* an idea for a new poem.

Later (until I changed it), "A Rose in Hell" became the title of a book for which Borges offered me a disturbing blurb, part of which was: "Three of the best things in America are Melville's whale, Barnstone's sonnets, and corn flakes." While I knew that each morning Borges ate corn flakes without milk for breakfast and really liked them, as he liked Northumberland or Spinoza's stars or a passage from Old English, I expressed reservations about listing cereal in that unlikely trinity. Whereupon he generously quipped, "Shall I add Emerson's intellectual poetry? Yes, I'll put in Emerson." Then, with increasing excitement, he went on adding early giants to that list of the best things in America: Dickinson, Hawthorne, Thoreau.

"No, the whale, Emerson, and corn flakes are more than enough," I answered hopelessly.

The only new poem I knew by Borges that had come directly out of our conversation had its origin on a plane we took together from Córdoba back to Buenos Aires. I was reading him poems in English— by Donne, Hopkins, and Frost. It seemed the most natural thing in the world to do on a plane with Borges. There have been few moments in my life that seemed equally irrevocable, central, where all else seemed trivial. On a plane with a blind Argentine poet. After reading "Birches," I mentioned that Frost's memory of swinging on and bend-ing down birch trees in New England was an unlikely if not impossible memory, a lie or a creation. Frost was born and spent his boyhood in California; when he moved to New England at ten, it was not to a Vermont or New Hampshire farm but to Lawrence, a mill city in Massachusetts. And if he did swing and bend birches into submission as a young adolescent ("So was I once myself a swinger of birches"), it was not as a farmboy who bent them ("As he went in and out to fetch the cows"), a country boy in his proper terrain as the poem suggests, but as a city boy visiting the country. I may have misinformed Borges about Frost; if so, so much the better, for on hearing this apparent discrepancy between Frost's biography and imagination, Borges's smiling teeth and dead eyes lit up and he said he had an idea for a poem.

"Do you have a title?"

" 'An Impossible Memory.' "

"What kind of poem? Formal or free verse?"

"Free verse. My Whitman variety."

"How long?"

"About forty lines."

A few weeks later Borges published in *La Nación* "Elegía del recuerdo imposible" (Elegy for an Impossible Memory), a poem of forty-two lines, with Whitmanian anaphora and sweep. That same year, 1976, it became the initial poem of his new collection, *La moneda de hierro* (The Iron Coin). The poet asks for the impossible memory of his mother gazing into the morning at her Santa Irene estate (she with no knowledge that her name was to be Borges); of the Danes sailing from Hengist for an island which was not yet England; of having heard Socrates in the afternoon of the hemlock, serenely examining the problem of immortality while death rose blue from his already cold legs; of the memory that "you had said you loved me and had not slept until dawn, torn apart and happy." All these impossible explorations derived from his discovery that Frost had invented an unlikely memory of swinging on birches.

"I'm calling from China."

"This must be an expensive chat."

"Would you like to visit China? I've arranged an invitation for you from the Chinese Writers' Union, and the Argentine ambassador will arrange for your and María's passage. Would you like to come?"

(Actually, from his writing and so many talks I knew that China was, like Japan, the site of a dream he needed to experience. He had gone to Japan a few years earlier, just after an operation for the removal of his prostate. He had been moaning about that operation. To me, and I suppose to others, he had said, "They unmanned me."

María Kodama had had enough bellyaching, and a few days after the invitation to Japan came, she gave Borges an ultimatum: either recover and be ready to leave in a week, or she would never accompany him to the Far East. Borges was visited, as it were, by the miraculous healer Yannis Kovernatos from medieval Crete, or the Renaissance Franciscan brother Hermano Pedro, who healed thousands in Antigua, Guatemala. By week's end Borges was fine and as enthusiastic as a child about Japan. It was one of his happiest trips. He especially liked the Japanese Zen priests. He said that during this whole trip everyone talked about essential things; never once did conversation degenerate into literary talk.)

"Of course I want to come to China," Borges said heatedly into the phone. "Do you think I would not want to go to China? Do you suppose me insane? Do you think I haven't read the *I Ching* and the *Tao Te Ching* and *The Dream of the Red Chamber*? Do you think I don't know Buddhist and Taoist scriptures or Kafka's 'The Great Wall of China' or the deeds of the Son of Heaven, Shih Huang Ti the Bookburner? Do you imagine I haven't studied the infinite labyrinth of the Yellow Emperor's palace?"

Consider Borges's many references to China in his work:

> I read, a few days ago, that the man who ordered the almost infinite wall of China to be built was that First Emperor, Shih Huang Ti, who likewise ordered all books antedating him to be burned. That these two vast undertakings—the five or six hundred leagues of stone thrown up against the barbarians, and the rigorous abolition of history, that is, of the past—should originate with the same person and be in some way his attribute, inexplicably pleased and, at the same time, disturbed me. The purpose of this note is to examine the reasons for that emotion. (*"The Wall and the Books,"* 89)

For Borges, China was many things—the Yellow Emperor, the fragrance and odors of class differences, the scholar and the criminal, the Taoist meditation on existence and the Kafkan researcher in penal cruelty, the search for a secret word for the universe for which the Chinese poet in the Emperor's palace, on the brink of revelation, would lose his head for having discovered omnipotent knowledge. But above all China was an attitude to an unknown truth, a mysterious event that is always about to be, but whose imminence is never understood.

"You have always been in China," I said to him.

"Of course I've been to China. Do you think I'm illiterate?"

"Not entirely. Maybe you suffer from some learning disabilities, would you say?"

"You're very generous."

"Not at all. I even suspect that deep down you are Chinese, an old disciple of Lao-tzu, perhaps his scribe. I suspect you have been stealing from Lao-tzu the way you have openly stolen the butterflies of Chuang-tzu. Anyway, let me stop blabbering to tell you that the Argentine ambassador, Subiza, will bring you an official invitation. How is María? Does she have the loneliness of the moon?"

"So you remember my quatrain to her. I have written only a few lines directly to her. Anneliese reproaches me for not doing more. She says, 'For twenty years María and I have worked together and just four lines for María.' I tell my German friend I'm shy, but she says I am stingy with my poetry."

"Anneliese is a woman of stern character, as a reader of your pessimist Schopenhauer should be. And she knows you inside out. But how is María?"

"I like María, and she puts up with me."

Our connection was exceptionally clear, much better than local calls in Beijing. It helped us forget distance and time. Already we were trading blows.

"But tell María not to work so hard for you. After all, you are only a minor writer. You say so yourself."

"I know it all too well. A minor writer. If, like Zola, I wrote about coal mines, I could call myself a "coal-minor" writer. Coal mines are more intricate, after all, than labyrinths. As you know, I don't keep a single volume of that minor author in my house."

"Yes, you're a terror with the works of Borges. I must say, you do keep up your modesty. It's effective against the temptation of arrogance. I think you have taken theological vows, which you adhere to without vacillation."

"Why, I am a very religious person. And I respect vows. Only I don't respect God—or, I should say, he is a linguistic presence in my mind and work, but I don't care for that figure if he does exist, and if he does it would be very disagreeable. I am looking forward to eternal peace. Pure peace. And I would not want to share it with such divine company. Of course, if others wish to, I compliment them. But God is not for me."

"I too don't care for that bully," I said. "But I don't look forward to extinction with the same resolution that you pretend."

"What can I do? Do you have a better end to things? Or beginning, if you wish?" he said in resignation.

"If God were someone else, or something else, with a better personality, it would help. But I'm afraid that's just talk, since I have not the slightest belief in, or even fear of, that transcendent figure. I can't even cope with how existence fell into my shoes, much less what the face of God looks like. As for fear, I have enough of that in those moments, still infrequent, when I think of extinction, which I do not relish. You told me once that you have to wake up each day to being Borges again. I wake up much of the time, at any time of day, surprised that I am myself, that being is in me."

"Willis, you should keep some aspirin handy for those very serious moments. I myself am now quite used to long waits alone, when I can really do nothing. Then I am forced to think, to remember friends, to work out puzzles—I used to be very into Bradley and the philosophers of my generation—and I have even enjoyed those moods. I welcome solitude, which was never the case when I was younger. But when I get too jumpy, I ask a friend to come over to read to me. It is a fine thing to be lost in another voice."

"Why don't you shock yourself by having someone read you one of your old stories? You might be very surprised."

"Well, yes, I am in serious fear I will be surprised, and I take guard against it. You can't blame me for protecting myself against Borges."

"You remind me of the Chinese emperor Shih Huang Ti, the great bookburner, your hero in 'The Wall and the Books.' You too are a Chinese bookburner, but you've chosen to burn the volumes of that public man, Borges. Maybe the private man, too. Yet, with all that, you sound less timid, as if you're gaining confidence and about to enter a promising period."

"Now, look here. Then there's some hope for me, wouldn't you say?"

"There's hope, but don't rush into print."

"I have not *rushed*," he protested. "I'm afraid I have galloped into print."

"You're lost, then. And the rest of us. We have to live with all that erudite trash you've been writing. But we're all waiting eagerly for someone to come along and publish *Pierre Menard, Author of the Complete Minor Works of Jorge Luis Borges.* We're counting on a civilized Frenchman to redeem the work of the barbarous blind Argentine. Take care. And I hope María will not let you get out of hand. She's your best self, the true Borges."

"Barnstone, you are too charitable with me, with the barbarous blind Argentine," he said, with the bantering lilt we had already fallen into.

When Borges began "to wield his modesty like a club," to use Alastair Reid's good-natured accusation, I would pick up on it, agreeing and even adding to his self-abuse, and at that point we traded blows and hyperboles and felt comfortable.

"You are the poet who strangely prefers Antonio," he went on.

"Of course. Like you, that Spaniard had much to be modest about. By the way, have you forgiven me for laughing at you, right in your face, that evening in the flat when you said, 'See you later, alligator'?"

"All your sins are forgiven," he uttered with gravity.

"Bishop Borges, I can't help taking you on. You seem to bring out my unpredictable — shall I say — awful side. But the 'sacred friendship,' as you would say, sticks. It's always old times, and you make me sentimental."

"Oh, not that. Hang on. Don't go so low. You'll end up like crybaby Lear walking about dreaming, with his dead daughter in his arms, thinking they're two birds in a cage."

"Is it that bad?"

"I'm pulling your leg, Willis."

"Pull away." Suddenly I remember we're on the phone. "Look here, I'd better not talk anymore. I'm becoming poor from all this excited chatter that's flying over oceans and continents down to you in Buenos Aires. It will be wonderful if you come to China, no? Do come to China. Goodbye, Borges."

"Goodbye, Barnstone. A Rose in Hell. Goodbye, Willis."

Borges hung up. Before I did likewise there was an electronic gargling, and the Chinese operator came on to ask if I were through with the communication.

"No," I said.

These were the last words I exchanged with Borges. We ended as we had began almost two decades earlier, in paradox, Borges spoofing, learned, with Cartesian logic and emotional depth. Somehow, lost on the phone, I felt as close to him as I had ever been. God, existence, literature. We centered on those incomplete, incompletable mysteries. This morning we were a little closer. But the true word, if it has a chance for truth, must never be uttered, never even conceived.

For all his masks, many do not recognize the immediacy and candor of Borges's emotional intelligence. Never have I known anyone so direct about the essentials—his fears, his loves, his skepticism, his idealism. At the same time, he doesn't make access to essentials cheap or shoddy. While his candor is direct, the listener may be required to decode his language, going along a way so often filled with paradox, humor, reversal, and all his anti-sentimental weapons.

When we first met in New York in 1968 I expressed admiration for the Spanish poet Antonio Machado, Machado el Bueno (Machado the Good) as he is sometimes called. Antonio's brother, Manuel, a minor poet, is sometimes referred to as El Malo (The Bad) in unjust comparison.

In good form, Borges said the unexpected: "If you are speaking of El Bueno, you mean, of course, Manuel."

"No, I mean Antonio," I protested.

"But Manuel is the great one and much more memorable," Borges countered. To prove his point he began to recite lines not from Manuel but from, yes, Antonio. He was particularly fond of the first stanza of Antonio Machado's well-known autobiographical poem, "Retrato" (Portrait), because of the allusion, in its fourth line, to the first line of the *Quijote*:

> Mi infancia son recuerdos de un patio de Sevilla
> y un huerto claro donde madura el limonero;
> mi juventud, veinte años en tierra de Castilla;
> mi historia, algunos casos que recordar no quiero.
>
> (My childhood is memories of a patio in Seville
> and a bright orchard where the lemon trees ripen;
> my youth, twenty years on the land of Castile;
> my life, a few events I care to have forgotten.)

The Argentine ambassador to China, Hector Subiza, delayed his return to Argentina. By the time Subiza went to see the poet, Borges's doctor would not let him take more than one speaking trip that year, and he was already committed to Austria. In the spring of 1985, after Subiza informed me of this situation, I was morosely disappointed. I supposed the doctor had his reasons, and, true, the Chinese Writers' Union had expressed concern about his health, about caring for the eighty-five-year-old poet during a rigorous month of travel and conferences. They feared, they told me, he might die on them. But I knew otherwise.

Borges never reached China, the place of a dream. Liver cancer killed him a year later. Yet in his final year Borges dictated those poems of deep pathos, including a meditation that appeared in English translation in *The New Yorker* a week before his death. In it he speculates about what city of the world he will die in. Until the end his roots, so Argentine, so distinctly fed in the Rio de la Plata barrios of Adrogué and Palermo, were also, like his writings, of the world. Had Borges come to China he would have thrived, and the Chinese who were with him would have thrived. He would leave his anonymous Spanish and English phrases to merge somehow—through conversation, *charlas,* translation, and rumor—into the spirit of the billion Chinese. The billion Chinese, in turn, would have instilled in Borges a new flowering.

Borges's earlier writings about China, like his romances in Averröes's Arab Orchard or about Kabbalah or in a Babylonian library or a pre-Columbian jungle, were dreams of erudition. The pirate widow Ching from *The Universal History of Infamy* reveals his special manipulation of historical facts or gossip. But to view a live China, I guessed that he would use the same lens of fantastic realism with which he observed the knife handler Juan Muraña in his hangouts in rough Buenos Aires neighborhoods, to describe mounds of white cabbage outside dank cement entryways, crowds of men in undershirts standing around in the drab yet exotic Beijing neighborhoods and, out in the spring hills around Chengde, the yellow Taoist temples. China would have been a major event in his life.

Given these notions, these dreams about Borges in China, during that last half-year in Asia I invented a Borges in China. As I rode my Flying Pigeon bicycle through back streets of Beijing and through the immense, shabby squares battered by winds carrying spring dust, fumes, and Gobi sand into my eyes, I thought of Jorge Luis Borges, whom now I knew I would not see in China. Yet I saw him there.

Earlier I had imagined moving about the country with him and María. María's infinite patience would be the norm in China. In an essay "On the Gnostics" Borges wrote, "Had Alexandria triumphed and not Rome, the extravagant and muddled stories that I have summarized here would be coherent, majestic, and perfectly ordinary" ("A Vindication of Basilides the False," 27). In China, María's discreet wisdom, her understatement and wry perceptions, along with her laughter, would be perfectly ordinary. Borges, fond of ancient ruins in the desert, of steep altitudes, twilights, and the grotesque, could have in spring or summer experienced both the low cities of the Gobi in Chinese Turkestan and, directly south, the almost airless blue and mustard plateaus of towering Tibet.

Now I concocted a Borges in many settings. I knew he would capture the Chinese — they have never lost their reverence for the sage. Who in the world would better fit the picture of Lao-tzu, Chuang-tzu or Confucius than the slow-walking blindman from Argentina?

Borges had an appointment with white clouds. I saw him conversing in Deep South Mountain with an old woodcutter, a man like himself except with good sight. They fell into conversation and were laughing, lost to time, forgetting about return until the dusk settled on them and on the desolate cane fences in the nearby village. The mountains, which were green and crooked, took on the mist that Borges always felt surrounded by, a result of his obscured vision. Now the whole landscape assumed his own vision of blue and yellow mists, and in agreement with the Buddhist principles he had interpreted for Western readers he became part of the mountain-over-water (the Chinese character for landscape) near classical Chang'an, the capital city of the Tang poets. He no longer looked at a mirror through the land to see himself. Rather, he was part of the Buddhist world mirror made of the entire land in which he was himself a speck of mirror reflecting outward — one among thousands of mirroring brooks and pine trees.

In his room at night he dictated new poems to María as he had done in Japan. Soon China became, like Japan, another island for the Argentine poet, a place of curved roofs, Sung enlightenment yellow tiles, and discourse.

From the bottom of the planet Borges had gone up to the non-barbarian center of the earth. China was perhaps another invention between *limbo* and *paradiso* of the Florentine Dante or a dream from Pascal's sphere whose center is everywhere. There he spent his last weeks, going from one chamber to another, one gateway and temple to another in the Mongol, Manchu, and Han configurations that became the Forbidden City, but which he had already drawn with nightmarish accuracy when in words and mind he invented his own labyrinths that were his atlas of hell, earth, and heaven.

One night in 1937 three friends, Jorge Luis Borges, Adolfo Bioy Casares and his wife, Silvina Ocampo, fell to talking about fantasies and ghost stories. They put their ideas into a notebook, out of which came *The Book of Fantasy* (a book recently published by Viking in English translation). In it Borges found Pao-yu, his friend from the eighteenth-century Chinese novel *The Dream of the Red Chamber,* lost in infinite dream.

Though they were still sitting around the same heavy worktable, Borges left his Argentine compatriots and drifted off into his own fantastic geographies. He was puzzled, for no sooner did he focus on Pao-yu (Precious Jade) in a flower garden surrounded and pampered by beautiful young women than he saw himself as the onlooker in the same garden—another Jorge Luis Borges staring at an identical Pao-yu lying senseless on a bed in a nearby garden. This Borges had just stepped outside from the mansion's red chamber, and as he looked at Pao-yu's double he was troubled and confused. Yes, Borges understood what had happened. The novel's real Pao-yu had dozed off. In his dream he found a young man on his bed in the garden, and he did embrace his double; but it was the real Pao-yu, squinting, making a funny face. He stopped only when his maid was yelling orders for him to go at once to his father's chamber. Even then he was dazed and confused, and accused of still dreaming, for he found himself calling to the dreamt Pao-yu, and he stopped only when his maid pointed out to him that he was looking not at the flower garden but at his own reflection in the mirror.

Now Borges, the onlooker of Pao-yu's dream, was outlandishly confused and even upset. How can I too have a double far over there in China? I am watching someone else's dream, I have seen him come out of it. What's going on? Who has discovered all this fantasy? Which one am I, and where am I?

Borges rubbed his eyelids. Looking more carefully through his not yet blind eyes he saw nothing. But then he felt an object a few feet in front of his face. He touched the surface, cold and smooth as a knife. As he moved his hands, he realized he was staring at his own puzzled reflection on the unseen depths of an iron mirror. Behind it lay orange temples delicately poised at the sky and shaped like calligraphy and meditation chambers amid the dung-smelling fields of China.

Suddenly he heard his Buenos Aires friends. Though still sitting at the table beside him, they seemed to be yelling at him from a great distance.

"Borges, you're still dreaming."

"I am seeing double," Borges protested. He was no longer confounded, but stubborn and happy. "My China and its gardens have multiplied. Don't bother me. I have waited a lifetime to come here. I have exploited every mist and nightmare to walk alone into these Chengde temples on the spring fields with their silent reapers. This is Xanadu, seven hours by train directly north of Beijing, where I have made an appointment with empty mountains, and you are disturbing my vision."

My Name Is Might-Have-Been

When Borges entered the real labyrinth, the original stone
one at Knossos, which has not departed from the Earth or
time, he entered together with María and became lost. In a
labyrinth one is lost; that is its purpose. But now he entered
in the morning with María and was not lost alone. María
took a photo of Borges sitting with his cane on the steps of
the maze. Four fingers of his hand show a useless compass,
pointing nowhere. But his blind eyes are wide open, looking
toward María and her lens.

I had no direct word about Borges until after my return
from China. One late afternoon in June 1986, driving with my son,
Robert, on the Pennsylvania Turnpike, pulling a trailer filled with
old Chinese furniture, we were listening to the news in the midst
of a fierce rainstorm. *Jorge Luis Borges, the Argentine writer, died
today in Geneva.* The signal was so weak I could barely hear the
words, but I knew their import would not be changed if they were
transmitted more clearly.

I had often mused that I would go down to Buenos Aires if Borges
died. He talked so often about death—he was always saying he
welcomed it, that he was weary of waking up to the dreary task of
another day of being Borges, and a lot of other understandably untrue
statements. Much of Borges's most profound writing concerns the
instant of death, the secret of the instant after death, the word in
this world that will explain the obscure script of the universe. Being
a declared unbeliever in the immortality of the body, spirit, or a
personal memory, he leads the reader to the articulation of the single
revelatory word, but always in the voice of some personage who will
disappear or die before uttering it.

In the earlier mentioned "Parable of the Palace" the poet, the
emperor's slave, found a word equal to the Yellow Emperor's palace,
worthy of every detail down to the design and light on each piece
of porcelain. The emperor had the executioner's iron sword cut the

poet down, for with that word the poet had robbed the emperor of his palace. The poet's descendants still seek, and will not find, the word to gain them the universe.

The same elusive word that reveals the universe, the universe at death, is the subject of Borges's famous "Conjectural Poem." Francisco Laprida, a relative of Borges through his maternal grandmother, reflects before he dies. He is about to see and to know everything:

> At last I've discovered
> the concealed key to my years,
> the fate of Francisco de Laprida,
> the missing letter, the perfect
> pattern that God knew from the beginning.
> In the mirror of this night I reach
> my unsuspected eternal face. The circle
> is about to close. I wait for it to be.

But as he is about to know, his death deprives the reader of what Laprida might articulate; by writing the poem in the first person, Borges lies behind Laprida, further suggesting that the poet seeks in the night's mirror his innocent eternal face and is himself deprived until that instant when the knife takes him into oblivion. The violence of death means absolute deprivation of the vital gnosis by which earthly life may be made explicit:

> Now the first blow,
> the harsh iron ripping my chest,
> the intimate knife across my throat.

Or in "In Praise of Shadow," the enigma of self-knowledge is to be revealed.

> From the South, the East, the West, the North
> the roads converge that take me
> to my secret center.

As the poem ends it seems that Borges will know:

> Now I can forget them. I reach my center,
> my algebra and my key,
> my mirror.
> Soon I will know who I am.

The speaker in the poem *will* know, but neither Borges nor the speaker will ever tell. When Borges died, of course he left no secret words for us. He would not, by an act or a word, betray our trust by giving us false coins. Whatever it means, we may repeat his words, uttered over and over again in the poems, "Soon I will know who I am." That he will know, even through the expected nothingness of extinction, is as close as he did and will come to revelation.

Obsessed as he was—and frustrated—by death's enigmas, seeking its meanings, inviting it, he did express them conversationally in his own parables. Once he told me that when a thief had held him up in a barrio, saying to him, "La bolsa o la vida" (Your purse or your life), he had replied, "La vida"—whereupon the thief turned on his heels and fled. Borges said, "I was disappointed. It might have been some kind of solution."

This conversation took place at the domestic airport in Buenos Aires in 1975, while we were waiting for the plane that was to leave nine hours late. I thought of all the times I had taken Borges to airports, had sat beside him on planes, listening to a man who rarely sat beside you without indulging, without respite, in literature. I thought of Maxim's restaurant in Buenos Aires, a modest place, and of the more elegant Saint James Café which was our late haunt. After an evening of discussion, reading, work, jokes, philosophy, Borges would say at midnight or later, "Why don't we see how things are at the Saint James?" And we would walk four or five blocks to our splendid refuge and resume our literary antics and human obsessions.

Often I read Wallace Stevens or Cavafy to him at the Saint James, and during one long Sunday morning breakfast there we spoke for hours about only Milton and Dante. We were speaking more quickly than usual, and there was not a moment's pause. Milton and Dante entered the morning of the world that day, their first day, and we had discovered them. His observations were extraordinary: spontaneous, brilliant, yet as if written out on a page with the greatest care. There was electricity in the air around the several images of Borges in the corner mirrors next to which we sat. Ultimately, Borges loved and learned more from Milton than from Dante; his own sonnets, even in their frequent specific references to Milton, prove this. And so, predictably, Dante seemed to come out better, as Borges's first poet of the world, as the poet who, unlike Milton, did not believe in any of those beautiful and absurd religious myths.

"It was because Dante didn't believe in his extravagant and fearful *Inferno* that it, and therefore his poem, are credible," he argued.

Rarely had I seen him so enthusiastic about a subject—though I should add that while I often saw Borges weary, pessimistic, even despondent, I never recall the least jadedness about him or his speech. Now he was pure eloquent energy.

By the time evening came, I began to feel a curious melancholy. We had gone back to his apartment for lunch, had worked together, and were about to leave the building to go to Maxim's for supper. Down in the ground-floor hallway, just before we stepped onto the broken pavement outside, I confessed that I was depressed.

"What makes you say that, Barnstone?"

I explained that that this morning at the Saint James I had been unusually happy. I felt rich then, and now deprived. While the ideas of our conversation remained in my mind, most of the phrases were already hazy; in some weeks, months, even the main turns of phrases and arguments would surely fade. After a few years I would remember only that we had had a remarkable discussion about Milton and Dante.

"I will remember your excited precision, perhaps some of those distinctions between the Protestant and Catholic poets," I said, "and maybe that my retorts were animated—but really none of the words."

I suppose I was greedy. It is said about so many of the wise and religious thinkers, including Greeks and East Indians, that words fixed on a page lose their breath—a notion of all the itinerant sages including Socrates, Jesus, the Buddha, and Lao-tzu. But such noble thoughts didn't wash, at least for me. The inadequacy of my memory and all the consequent loss of specific words deeply upset me. Our conversation was real, like theater; there were summits, we stayed up there for hours, and now it was over. We came down and the scene became vague, almost gone. (In 1990, as I record this conversation of 1975, I remain utterly convinced of the importance, of the insights of our conversations, although only two certain words remain in my memory: Milton and Dante.)

Borges put his arm around my shoulder and puzzlingly, with paradoxical consolation, said, "Remember what Swedenborg wrote—that God gave us a brain so we might have the capacity to forget."

A few days later, on Christmas night, in an atmosphere of civil tension, Borges and I shared a Christmas dinner at an English lady's apartment. Borges was very grave. We ate good food, drank good wine, and talked, but the underlying national gloom was on our minds. The morgues and hospitals were filled with the bodies of young Argentine men and women, largely students, who had taken part in a massive attack on a central police station. The police had been tipped off and it was a slaughter. Up in Tucumán there was open-field fighting. But the violence from the opposition was almost over. In a few months the military would take over completely and the wave of *desaparecidos,* already enormous, would become the Dirty War.

Supper and liqueurs over with, it was time to go. Since there was a bus and taxi strike, we had to walk. Borges, always sensitive to good manners, insisted on first accompanying María Kodama home, although she lived at the opposite end of the large city. But this was not a burden to the blind seventy-six-year-old poet, for he loved to walk, especially at night, and it gave him an excuse for conversation. In that windy, alert half-light we slowly crossed the city. As the hours passed Borges seemed more and more awake to every oddity in the streets, to the architecture which his blind eyes somehow knew, to the few passersby. Suddenly a bus appeared and María hopped on it, and we headed back to Borges's flat.

Now that María was, we hoped, safely on her way home, there was no way of hurrying Borges. At first I thought he might not know his way, for he stopped every few steps when he made some important point and circled about his cane as if we were lost. But no, he wanted to talk about his sister, Norah, and their childhood, about the gaucho he saw shot on the Brazil-Uruguay border some forty years earlier, and about his military ancestors who fought in the nineteenth-century civil wars.

"Who shot the gaucho?" I asked.

"Another gaucho, a black man. The two of them had some kind of minor dispute. It happened right in front of my eyes. They were standing as close to me as I am to you. But what impressed me most was that he killed the man casually, as if it were nothing at all. As if he were unbuttoning his shirt."

When Borges spoke of civil wars, he meant the struggles between liberal *unitarios,* whom his ancestors had fought with, and the *federales* under the dictator Rosas. His maternal great-grandfather, Colonel Isidoro Suárez, was the hero at the famous battle of Junín in the

Peruvian highlands. But the single figure of his personal mythology was Colonel Francisco Borges, his paternal grandfather, who at a ball to celebrate a victory against a gaucho militia met and fell in love with an Englishwoman, Frances Haslam. It was 1870 or 1871. That afternoon, from the flat roof of her house, Fanny had watched her future husband riding at the head of his regiment to defend the city of Paraná (*Aleph*, 204–5).

From Fanny Haslam, his Northumbrian grandmother, Borges received a line to the English language as well as the common genes that were to leave her, his father, and himself blind in the last decades of their lives. However, it was the extraordinary drama of the young Colonel Borges's last afternoon on the field, a historical and family tale of honor and death, that haunted Borges. He wrote about it in at least two poems and in his autobiographical essay. He referred to it frequently in public lectures. He told me the story at an airport, in his apartment, once in a restaurant after we had spent an afternoon with the newspaper owner Mitre. He was a descendant of General Bartolomé Mitre, who had ordered the retreat at the battle of La Verde, a retreat which Colonel Borges protested through his death. Now, in greater detail, as if for the first time, Borges recounted this episode, with strange emotion, in an unnamed small plaza in Buenos Aires an hour before dawn.

The battle at La Verde was going poorly, yet Colonel Borges was convinced that the enemy was about to run out of firepower. General Mitre ordered the troops to fall back. It was almost dusk on November 26, 1874. When the battle was over, Francisco Borges mounted his horse and rode out slowly, wearing a white poncho, followed by a few of his men. His arms were folded across his chest. As they neared enemy lines, there was a crackle of rifle fire; the colonel fell, two Remington bullets lodged in his stomach. He died two days later.

"It was a form of suicide, you know," Borges said.

> I leave him on his horse in the half-light
> Of dusk in which he sought his death;
> From all the hours of fate, may this one,
> Bitter and overwhelming, endure.
> The whiteness of his horse and poncho
> Moves over the terrain. Patient death
> Lurks in ambush in the rifles. Sadly

Francisco Borges crosses the plain.
("Allusion to the Death of Colonel
Franciso Borges, 1833–1874")

"He had to do it. It was a statement of defeat and protest. His actual words, two days later, were plainly rhetorical, and less to the point: 'I have fallen in the belief of having fulfilled my duty and my convictions, and for the same principles I have fought all my life.' That was the obligatory utterance. Every Spartan who died at Thermopylae knew the formula. As for suicide: it is a young man's act or a very old man's gesture of weariness. Then, of course, there is the military for whom death is an easy, inevitable, and foolish resolution."

Since my family seemed to carry suicide as his did blindness, we were often moved to talk about those who open the false door of self-inflicted death. Borges complained about being condemned to onrushing time, to being Borges, even to the duty of living on into what one day might be the physical punishment afflicted on his mother in her great age. Yet these complaints were misleading. For wisdom never made him blasé, and there was never a time when he was not still a child with centuries of life before him, vast oncoming time which he awaited and indulged in eagerly. Despite the loneliness and isolation inherent in blindness, Borges lived truly for that Bradleyan onrushing future. While he infused his writing with real and invented scholarship and history, he was apparently satisfied, even intent, on downgrading his own earlier books and days and filling his mind with those books he was planning to write, those places he would visit, those friends he would see again. Schopenhauer notwithstanding, his convictions about metaphysical darkness were, in typical paraodox, refuted by his irrepressible élan, by the virtually inexhaustible vitality of his actions and projects.

So we talked away the darkness.

Often his cane hit a hole or small ditch in the broken pavement. Each small event offered him the chance to pause, to stretch his cane, to extend his arms and legs in the posture of an actor and go off on a new tack. Out of context, he talked about his fondness for swimming, about women he had cared for in his youth, how his mother had learned to cook in Austin, Texas, and of walks he used to take under those "electric moons" hovering on high towers over the center of the Texas city. Then we went back further, to his adolescence, when, full of anticipation, he strolled inquisitively about the streets of old Palermo.

"The Italian immigrants in those days we called *gringos.* They were the first people I saw doing the tango. That new dance with the interesting bad words, and I saw them not in a dance hall or a bar or on stage but in the street in front of the whorehouses in the barrio of Palermo. Not mixed couples but men I saw, dancing with each other. They were practicing at the street corner to give themselves courage before going inside to dance with the women."

I began to spot the first milk trucks. As always, I felt that Borges's character and talk were at least as profound and elegant as his writing and because of this confirmed writing itself. By dawn we had reached his building. He took out his chain of keys, fumbled through them with distracted care, and finally, in a sigh of reluctant duty, came upon the right one. Another long night of conversation was over.

How could I return to Argentina, the country now empty of Borges?

For years I had pressured Borges as well as his Argentine editor, Carlos Frías, to pay María a modest salary so she would not have to wake at 5:30 each morning to give Spanish lessons to Japanese businessmen in order to spend the rest of her day and weekends taking dictation from Borges, reading to him, and accompanying him on his trips. But Frías simply never had the vision, and Borges was equally blind. He would say he would like to pay María a salary for her work but "she's proud as Punch and would never accept." María, for her part, would have gladly accepted and abandoned the dawn-tutored Japanese businessmen; but, yes, "proud as Punch" she would say nothing to Borges.

María was born in Argentina of a German mother and a Japanese father, a very austere chemist who had never let her weep since early childhood. Once, when she was three or four years old, she did weep. Her father picked her up, shook her, and admonished her severely, saying no decent person sheds tears. Since then she couldn't, she told me ruefully. I always took a cultural view—not an ugly one—of María's situation. I thought no Spanish-Italian Argentine would put up with the hardship, almost servitude, of attending to all Borges's literary, logistical, and many other needs. Only a Japanese or one imbued with extraordinary values of loyalty and fortitude could do so.

Eventually some of us who arranged trips for Borges insisted that María be given at least one-third of the honorarium for being there. We often arranged for her also to give lectures. Although María has her doctorate in Old English language and literature from the University of Buenos Aires, she was unable to teach because her schedule depended on Borges's journeys in Argentina and abroad. She was at least able to write and publish a collection of her own remarkable narrations, very original stories of the fantastic, bearing no discernible trace of Borges's hand.

At one point lovely María told me that sometimes she was so fed up she could hardly breathe. Having been extended offers by several Japanese universities, one day she announced to Borges that she would be going to Japan for two years to take a post at a university. Borges smiled and answered immediately, outrageously, "De modo que un poeta argentino, nacido en el año 1899, irá a vivir y morir en el Japón" (So that an Argentine poet, born in 1899, will go to live and to die in Japan). With that María knew there was no way out. Soon afterward her luggage was stolen from a New York hotel lobby. It contained her address book and all correspondence with Japan.

When Borges and María went together to a formal occasion, they were an extraordinary pair. Borges, caning into a room, a lobby, an auditorium, holding onto María's arm, dominating every environment. María serene and alert, severe in her care. Borges, often gazing out or up with his dead eyes to take in the new setting, always ready to return any remark that any of the unknown figures in the ever twilight of his vision would throw at him.

In Buenos Aires someone might stop him and say, "Borges, you are immortal."

"Sir, don't be such a pessimist."

After a lecture or chat, Borges was mobbed. María would stand by, patient and high minded, with no apparent distress while the hysteria continued. The truth was that Borges liked the immense attention and enjoyed signing books. One Sunday morning, after a stroll in Buenos Aires, he asked me to take him to a few bookstores and not to mention to each owner that he had been to the other's shop. We were on Corrientes Street and Borges was discoursing on *lunfardo* (a rich, amusing, lowlife Buenos Aires dialect with many Italian loan words, sometimes in tango lyrics, always on the lips of my *portero*), on the Academia de Lunfardo, which for Borges was the wonderful anti-Christ of pompous academies, and on *platense* speech, the speech of the whole basin of the Rio de la Plata. A gypsy woman came up to us and asked for money. I gave her a coin, the only one I had. She complained of its little value. Borges feigned indignation, saying, "After all, she shouldn't look a gift coin in the mouth."

At one bookstore, Borges fell into talk about Jesus on the Cross. "Not a very dignified death. Imagine asking God for help at the very last moment. His companions, the thieves—at least they were silent. Maybe the Scripture author preferred them to Jesus, for he had them plead for nothing. But Socrates: just compare the sentimental Jesus with Socrates, who had the finest death in history."

"Just compare the sentimental Jesus with Socrates, who had the finest death in history"—that sentence haunted me. Later I was to think about that dissident Jew, the *Rabbi* Jesus. In the koine Greek, Mary refers to her son as *rabbi,* though *Master* Jesus is the routinely political translation of *rabbi,* in order to conceal the fact that the man who died on the cross was a Jew. Yet precisely because he acted with weakness on the cross, with despair, I felt his humanity more. I would like to be able to argue that point with Borges today. Despite his occasional show of *machismo,* his fondness for knives, knife fighters and "streetcornermen," Borges was also the frail man tapping with his cane, courageous spiritually and with a natural compassion for weakness—and not only for those who might fear pain. His compassion took in the weakness of disenchantment with the absolute, the weakness of one who knows the limitations of words, of knowledge, who knows the futility of understanding and the frailty of his own resources to decipher the silence below language. Though others might mistakenly consider his resources superior, he left to others a discourse with God and eternity. Such words of transcendence were not his. He was left with a brooding intelligence of worldly limitations, as well as with the fortitude of reconciliation to things, even in dreams, for what they are. Given the tricks of existence, he could laugh at it, and did so all his life. He was not the Colonel Borges of his poems. As he grew older his poems took on an immense pathos precisely

because the speaker, Borges, was the weak man talking, the dreamer and despairer, unashamed to being the frightened blindman alone in the universe, measuring time with nightmares and metaphysical verses.

As for Jesus Christ, Borges was not of one mind in regard to those last moments when, as compared to Socrates, Jesus broke, groaned, and even called out for help. It was precisely that Jesus whom Borges wrote about and cared for — the pathetic sufferer, the frail human on the cross. In keeping with that vision is "Christ on the Cross," one of his last poems, in which he describes the insect-molested black-bearded Jew, broken, quietly suffering as a man, not a god. He is about to die, as countless others thereafter, including Borges, will suffer and die, all to no known purpose or hope for anything but extinction. The utter realism of that bloody martydom he depicts as an icon fated to inexorable repetition according to a very broad historical pattern in "John 1:14":

> The oriental histories tell a tale
> Of a bored king in ancient times who, fraught
> With tedium and splendor, went uncaught
> And secretly about the town to sail
> Amid the crowds and lose himself in their
> Peasant rough hands, their humble obscure names;
> Today, like that Muslim Harun, Emeer
> Of the true faithful, God decides to claim
> His place on earth, born of a mother in
> A lineage that will dissolve in bones,
> And the whole world will have its origin
> With him: air, water, bread, mornings, stones,
> Iris. But soon the blood of martydom,
> The curse, the heavy spikes, the beams. Then numb.

"Borges, here you are sitting next to me, taking coffee in the front of this bookstore. Everywhere — in life, history, literature — people are being born and dying..."

"No, no, no! Don't go on. You must not use those abstruse words, *life, history, literature, people.* I don't think I can take them in. I don't think I should take them in, difficult and elusive as they are. And I can't conceive of *everywhere* and *everybody.* Those are words, just words. Worse, words with little real meaning to my mind. I can believe in single people but not in those vague statistical crowds. (I almost said clouds.) I can believe in Jesus, a Jew who probably existed, who was executed miserably (as was the habit of his time, and of ours), and about whom later on all kinds of magical stories were invented. It happens with all our mythical heroes, but usually we don't see the process so clearly. Once they enter literature, it is their own world, and they cease having a real history. Do we know what Hamlet studied in Germany or Holland? That's only for a few academics, it's irrelevant and not for readers, since literary figures really don't have a historical time outside their verbal incarnation. Whatever their origins outside books, they exist only once in print, and perhaps then forever, but not anything in between. Being held in by words, by literature, they cannot even die."

"A while ago I witnessed a personal death, a literary man, and all too real," I said to him. "There are single deaths. It was my closest friend. They were giving him strong doses of morphine, but it didn't quiet his tongue. He taught me in those last days. The lessons were not terrible. Even in his dying I am indebted to this Irishman."

"The Irish use their tongues the way an Eskimo uses his paddle."

"He was hanging on by a hair in the hospital, and when the priest —he didn't care much for him—offered his hand, he took it graciously and said to him, 'I'm just testing your grip.' The priest said, 'You're cheerful this morning.' The Irishman, 'You too. It's our common gallows humor.' Then he turned to the nurse and said, 'I presume on you, and I apologize, but I suppose that's your profession. Could you give me some chocolate ice cream?' It was about all he could eat, but he enjoyed it obsessively."

"Do I know that Irishman?"

"You should have. You missed him. He was a walking poem, he carried an inlaid Turkish cane, was a *caballero,* the kindest one I've known, with a Hell's Kitchen gruff voice. In those last days it was a struggle for him to speak. I was phoning his hospital room, and said, 'Thomas, how are you?' He told me, 'I'm flat on my back and misshapen.' That was the closest thing I heard to a complaint. 'Should I come over?' 'Be guided by your own lights,' he told me. I went in the early evening. He was asleep, drugged, but the nurse woke him for his pills. It was then he mumbled something about God's hands and mercy. Then he cheered up and said we should all go to Paris together. He went out suffering and laughing, and had the finest death in history."

"Yes, it has happened that way before. Mine will be the happiest."

"You are lucky. Lucky Borges."

"I am lucky because I will be extinct. At last I will not be Borges."

"That is a perversely disguised suicide," I said gruffly. "But thank God I've learned not to believe you."

On his trips abroad with María, Borges thrived on new places, friends, the surprises of the question-and-answer format, and the adulation. He fed his writing on what he "saw" on voyages — "I'm blind but I see," he would say — on those journeys to the islands of England, Manhattan, Japan, Iceland. In Buenos Aires, where he did most of his writing, he often complained to me of boredom, of inadequate stimulation, of the disuse of his English, which became passive and bookish. But Borges's complaints usually concerned those things he loved most, including Buenos Aires. Some of his notorious complaints were against James Joyce, and about *Don Quijote* in Spanish. (He declared once, for the sake of shock and paradox, that he had first read *Don Quijote* in English translation and ever after he had felt the *Quijote* in Spanish was an inadequate translation from the English — an idea echoed ironically in *Pierre Menard,* a pioneer work of literary theory.) And finally there were his misgivings about the Spanish language itself.

None of these declarations, strictly speaking, reflected anything more than a circle of protective rejection around elements he revered. His significant feelings about Joyce are reflected not in confessions to friends, perhaps momentarily true, but in his critical writings about Joyce, or in a stunning sonnet where in a few words he caught the essence of the writer. As for the *Quijote,* he once confided in me that he actually read it first, as an adolescent, in Spanish. I'm sure this is true. And perhaps no figures are more prevalent in his later poetry than Alonso Quijano, the impoverished country gentleman who became the dreamt-up knight, the Caballero of the Sad Countenance, and the failed author of them all, Miguel de Cervantes, with whom Borges identified most clearly. Borges spoke of heroes, but he preferred the down-and-outs, the outcasts and failed authors among whom he proudly counted himself. That double of Quijano and Quijote, in which one dreams up the other, and Borges dreams up both, goes on in a Borgesian progression, for in the end Quijote dreams up his ultimate maker, Cervantes, fighting, being wounded at Lepanto.

So we have Borges evoking Cervantes who invented Quijano who invented Quijote who again invents his literary master Cervantes, not as a writer but as the naval officer who fought valiantly in a sea battle off the coastal city of Lepanto (Naufpontos), Greece, where he was severely wounded, lost the use (for life) of his left arm, and insisted on being carried up on deck to continue his Quixotic fencing. So we have the familiar Borgesian mixture of loser, madman, dreamer, hero, writer, the articulate "Man of Glass," removed from his cot of straw and stood up at the corner to speak parables of dream and wisdom to the crowds through his fragile ready-to-shatter frame:

Alonso Quijano Dreams

The man awakens from a confusing bed
Of dream of scimitars and coastal land.
He scratches beard and forehead with his hand,
Wondering if he is wounded or is dead.
Will all those sorcerers who put a curse
On him — under the moon — keep plaguing him?
Nothing. Almost no cold. Only a dim
Sorrow from recent years that were adverse.
The knight was dreamt up by Cervantes or
Else Don Quijote was the dreaming knight.
The double dream bewilders them: the sight
Of something happening from long before.
Quijano sleeps and dreams. Dreaming a battle,
Dreaming the seas, Lepanto, and the shrapnel.

Borges was cheerfully misleading and self-contradictory, in the spirit of his favorite Walt Whitman's proud declaration of self-contradiction and containment of multitudes. His ultimate contradiction was perhaps his complaints about the Spanish language, which he loved, invented, and used like few others — at the very moment he might be excoriating it.

"In English I can say, 'I dream my life away.' The mere addition of a preposition gives a nuance for which there is no equivalent in Spanish."

Early in his career he was accused of not writing like an Argentine, of writing Spanish as one imposing a foreign syntax. Like a skilled karate artist, Borges would flow with the thrust, agreeing totally and using the blow to undo the opponent.

"Condemned as I am to Spanish, I try to liven it up," he would say, gleefully.

In reality, Borges was the master of modern Spanish; like Quevedo, he was adept at discovering its Latin roots, was involved in its history and in creating a personal tongue. His example has profoundly altered a generation of magic realists and fantasy writers from Julio Cortázar to Gabriel García Márquez, as well as myriad foreign writers from John Barth and Donald Barthelme to Mark Strand. But whether he received his methods from Old English, Kafka, Whitman, or Emerson (the latter was one of his intellectual heroes, underestimated in his opinion, and therefore never subjected to the love-rejection process of his other heroes and models), Borges remained Borges — not Kafka, Joyce, Cervantes, or even Stevenson. He invented himself and his ever changing idiolect.

Like Pasternak, Yeats, and other careful authors, Borges was obsessed with the problem of self-imitation, of becoming a mannerist of himself. He refused to keep copies of his own books, to reread his own stories and poems. By his last years, he had not reread his most famous stories in forty years. He often rejected his illustrious early writing as insolently baroque and pretentious compared to his later work, which María Kodama describes as "not simplicity, which is meaningless, but a shy and secret complexity" (Kodama, "Oriental Influences," 181). Pasternak similarly decried his early experimental poetry — surely his finest — as he sought quieter, plainer, more direct statement. Had Borges reread his writing more, he might have repeated himself less, but like any very special memory, which his father had advised him *not* to recall if he wished to keep it intact and uncontaminated, Borges kept his earlier writing free.

An exception was his first collection of poems, *Fervor of Buenos Aires,* which went through many revisions, and which he sometimes said was the source and statement of all his later writing.

Borges could be dramatic in his wavering view of his own work. Initially he left his first self-published book of poems in the pockets of overcoats hanging in the hall, garments belonging to members of the Buenos Aires Writers' Club. Later he combed through bookstores, buying up any remaining copies of the same book so he would not have the public shame of being associated with them. These youthful gestures and later attitudes of rejection were belied by his full belief in the worth of his work. Like Constantine Cavafy, whom I would read to him night after night in Buenos Aires, in Greek and in English, Borges knew who he was and what his work was. Once, in my presence, he acknowledged his worth as a writer. It was a summer meal in January 1976. Indignant about a slight from some Peronist organization, he argued that he was after all the leading author of Latin America. These words he told me in a confidential voice, as if to imply it was nothing he would say to the world. Even so, it was unlike Borges to offer any such self-appraisal, true as it was. His silence normally revealed only that it was unnecessary to say what was confidently understood.

In the end nothing Borges said or wrote about himself as a writer was to affect his work. Doubts, modesty, arrogance — none of that mattered. Borges was simply committed to writing, to making books; the extension of memory and the imagination was his definition of a book. Nothing was to deter him from the search for experienced truths through words. He never stopped. The poems written in his eighty-seventh year are among his most skilled, profound, and moving. His vision grew sharper, his hand surer still. He began in poetry and ended in poetry. Like the pre-Socratics, particularly "El Griego," his name for Heraclitus the Obscure, he wrote philosophy in verse and maxims, and his song was constant.

If paradox and contradiction seem to dominate many of his convictions and statements, Borges was the first to accept that dialectic. In a lecture on "El libro" (The Book) given at the University of Belgrano, Borges advised readers not to read secondary texts (that is, criticism) but to go directly to the orginal author. Then, realizing that in proof of his admonition he had been citing his favorite critics, Emerson and Montaigne, he stated his pure Whitmanian credo: "I am going to contradict myself, what does it matter if I contradict myself?" (Borges oral, 24).

To return in memory to those mob scenes where Borges, back in the city of his birth, signed books, shook hands, and exchanged wise pleasantries. For María these happenings were sometimes pleasant, more often tedious, yet she always acted with astute intuition and grace. Among the crowd of Borges admirers were inevitably some who behaved in hysterical, unpredictably painful ways, and not without overt hostility toward her. María was a person to flatter as an avenue to Borges. Yet who was this contemptuous shadow blocking their way? She was Borges's extremely genial and enigmatic Lazarillo—but few acted normally in her presence.

When the public part was over, we would have supper, usually a very late meal. Then María would chat with Borges in his room for an hour or so about the day. When the poet had gone to bed, María and I would often talk for a few more hours, even though she might have to wake up very early and go off for the next event. Sometimes she spoke of feelings of oppression, of the burden, pressures, and the absence of a life of her own. At such moments this mature woman was both the child and savior of Borges.

One evening, after going to a film together in Buenos Aires, María told me how she came to meet Borges. There had been some childhood acquaintance. But one day she had enrolled in Borges's Anglo-Saxon class at the University of Buenos Aires. After the first meeting she was curiously upset and told her friends she was dropping the course. Why? they asked. Because Borges was too great a person for her, María Kodama, to study under. Her friends tried to convince her of the foolishness of her thoughts, and they did succeed in persuading her that it would be rude to drop the course without first speaking to Professor Borges. The ploy worked. After the weekend she went to the next class and informed Borges of why she was dropping out. Of course, Borges would hear nothing of it, and for the next twenty years she was hooked.

Borges was curious about María's looks. She had often told him, he said, that she was very ugly. Younger and less secure than Borges, that mixture and game of pride and modesty was more severe for her; hence her mendacious words about her bad looks. She was at the time more reserved but less shy than her companion, and I never saw her lose her composure.

Borges asked me on several occasions what she really looked like and I always answered in the same way: "María is beautiful by any standard. And you are lucky she is willing to look at you."

He was very pleased.

One evening, in my apartment on Paraguay Street, Borges and María were at the door. My books were spread over the floor. I had been up the previous night reading and writing and had not cleared the mess away. Earlier in the afternoon, I had gone over with Borges a list of subjects that he would be willing to lecture on at Michigan State, where he was soon to spend an unhappy period. He asked me to call to reduce the number of lectures from ten to five. It was much more sensible; we went over a new list. Then, as we stood out in the hall, our last conversation drifting down the stairway, Borges looked very gallant and María chic and happy.

I said, "María, que linda pareces esta noche!" (María, how beautiful you seem tonight!)

A gentleman, Borges immediately objected. "María no parece linda. Lo es! (María doesn't seem beautiful. She *is* so!)

Of those many hot summer December evenings when we read and talked in Borges's flat, I remember one with peculiar nostalgia. It became a key to later Borges events. After supper we went back to look at Kipling. I was not particularly a convert to Kipling's poems—except for some of the *Barrack-Room Ballads*—or to Swinburne's lyrics, which Borges intoned at the drop of a hat. He was unrelenting in his love for a few poets and fiction writers born in the mid- and late nineteenth-century, among whom Swinburne, Stevenson, Kipling, Twain, Chesterton, and Wells were foremost. They were not his great early peaks, his Melville and Hawthorne, his Whitman, Poe, and Dickinson; but particularly Kipling and Wells he saw as his immediate masters and almost contemporaries. For them he reserved an intimate affection and respect. He also enjoyed his cranky position of support for the Victorians, proudly articulated, knowing perfectly well that modernism, which he had been central in forming, had largely, even aggressively, rejected their esthetic.

Borges asked me to take a book from the shelf. He knew the location of all his most esteemed books, and he could shuffle over to the library and finger the shelf until a desired volume responded to his touch. I read poems from his favorites for about ninety minutes. I should say we read them in chorus, for, with his teeth shining wide in a Fernandel smile, he happily repeated each poem as I read it. He knew them all by heart.

Borges's books, the books of others, were his life and his mirror. The mirror, one of his favorite yet terrifying objects, tells the truth even when he looks blindly at it and sees nothing, for then it hopelessly reveals the truth of his blindness. In contrast, his books (and not the ones he has written) are not limited to the immediate present; rather, they form a truly timeless mirror, not restricted by the moment of his glance. He has only to look at those books to stimulate his memory or have them read to him to renew it. Then, perhaps, those dead voices will keep searching for and telling him the essential words, if he can understand them. So in "My Books," from *La rosa profunda,* we hear:

My books (which don't know I exist)
Are as much a part of me as this face
With gray temples and gray eyes
I look for hopelessly in the mirror
And over which I run my hollow hand.
Not without the logic of bitterness
I think the essential words
Expressing me are in those leaves
That don't know who I am, not in those I've written.
It's better that way. The voices of the dead
Will go on always telling me.

I have referred to Borges's labyrinthine memory. One evening later in that spring of 1976, at my house in Bloomington, he was talking to a friend, Matei Calinescu. When Borges discovered that Matei was Romanian, he mentioned having read the work of an obscure Romanian woman novelist a while ago in Geneva. In 1916. She wrote in French. In one poem in a pseudofolkloric style, she had interspersed in the French text a few untranslated Romanian words that he had not understood. Would he be willing to explain their meaning to him?, he asked Calinescu. Then, as if reading from a page, he recited the longish rhyming insignificant ballad that he had read through in his teens.

Borges was not unaware of his prodigious memory. At another time at Columbia a student asked Borges if he had really created any original characters in his fiction.

"No."

"What about Funes, the Memorious?" the student responded.

"Yes, Funes. Well, that's me, and all the others with different names are perhaps one person, or variations of the same person. I am a man of limited imagination. You see, I have created one character, that poor nightmarish creature, Funes, who couldn't sleep, think clearly, or find peace. Because he could forget nothing."

When I put Kipling back on the shelf, Borges instructed me. "Look on the last page of the book, next to the cover."

I looked and found my telephone number.

"I put your number in my favorite book. Now let's take a walk."

We took the steps because there was no electricity in the hall.

"Did you know," he commented slyly, "Buenos Aires is the only city in the world where the elevator was invented before they discovered the stairway? But elevators work here only when they are *descompuestos* (out of order). Since this one is not *descompuesto,* tonight we walk."

María had just come over for a few minutes, and now, as we circled down quickly, she and I were stumbling about. Borges, used to the darkness, was perfectly at ease, floating to the street level like a shadowy young prince. On the ground floor, after tripping down seven flights of stairs through darkness, we were out of breath. I accused Borges of being a physical monster for still breathing serenely.

"Forgive me. I'm afraid I've gone beyond the age of panting."

Out in the street we circled the Plaza San Martín in front, bid goodbye to María, then went up Paraguay to the Saint James. I read him, as usual, a few poems by Wallace Stevens. When I read him Stevens's short poem, "The Reader," he was pleasantly stunned and said with unaffected humility: "If in my life I could have written a poem like that."

Then I started reading Stevens's "Sea Surface Full of Clouds." He stopped me abruptly after ten or twelve lines, and with the unjust contempt and perhaps jealousy he normally reserved for Federico García Lorca, whose work he knew poorly, he said, "Mere color," dismissing the work of the poet who a moment earlier had elicited his reverence.

At this point I began to pummel him with "essential" questions.

"You speak of being happy and also distressed. In your writing the tragic view is always framed in parody and irony, but when you talk to me your distress is without irony. First, I want to ask you, what truly makes you happy?"

"Why, I was truly happy when you were reading me the poems of Kipling," he pronounced with candor. He smiled as if he were again enjoying that pleasure.

"And what are some of those awful things you say you have done that have made you anguished—or even miserable?"

I expected a comment related to his recurrent fundamental nightmares, which, like childhood mirrors, were a source of terror.

"Well, I got married."

There was no trace of humor in his one-liner. He was grave and indignant. I thought of all his marriages, apart from the disastrous official one in the early 1970s. These were not to wives but to attentive men and women who, during his thirty years of blindness, protected him, managed him, imprisoned him. Being timid (to use his word) and by nature and conviction polite (despite a few outbursts of quite paranoid temper), he frequently found himself saved, manipulated, and ultimately incensed by devoted friends—until he would break free and see the protector no more. He moved from gentleness and gentility to severity. And then, along with complaints of loneliness, he enjoyed his freedom.

During the ten years after our exchange, I often considered Borges's response. "I got married." At the other extreme of family webs, he was absolutely devoted to his father, who died in 1938; and he was equally devoted to his mother, who died at the age of ninety-nine, sick and punished by God, she said to him, by being forced to endure so long. His mother, for three decades his surrogate wife and rival of his brief lawful spouse, died in 1975. It was a terrible death. Borges told Monegal that "she begged the maid to come and throw her into the garbage can. For the last two years her moaning and cries could be overheard even over the phone. When the end came, she was reduced almost to the bare bones, held together by only a film of parched skin, like a mummified image of herself" (474). In the summer after her death, Borges composed a poem of pathos and disappointment, "Remorse":

> I have committed the worst sin of all
> That a man can commit. I have not been
> Happy. Let the glaciers of oblivion
> Drag me and mercilessly let me fall.
> My parents bred and bore me for a higher
> Faith in the human game of nights and days;
> For earth, for air, for water, and for fire.
> I let them down. I wasn't happy. My ways
> Have not fulfilled their youthful hope. I gave
> My mind to the symmetric stubbornness
> Of art, and all its webs of pettiness.
> They willed me bravery. I wasn't brave.

> It never leaves my side, since I began:
> This shadow of having been a brooding man.

I considered Borges's ties of filial love, his revulsion at ensnaring bonds, and finally his most esteemed category of human intercourse, the one enduring territory: friendship. In this precinct there have been so many — Rafael Cansinos Assens, Alfonso Reyes, Macedonio Fernández, Paul Groussac, Victoria Ocampo, Emir Rodríguez Monegal, Alicia Jurado, Anneliese Von der Lippen, Adolfo Bioy Casares, among others. His closest friend, of course, was María Kodama.

It was María who gave Borges life for more than twenty years. Their unique friendship grew like seeds thrown onto earth of astonishing fertility. María was the one friend on whom Borges became truly reliant, but who in those decades of dependence never caged him. She read to him, took dictation for his poems, fictions, and essays, made travel arrangements, accompanied him, unobtrusively ordered his food and cut up his meat and vegetables, all while carrying on an interested conversation. She was at his lectures and interviews. She did everything but think and speak for him — as sometimes others had attempted to do. In every act there was an equipoise of authority and discretion, of skill and good feelings. It was she, on the contrary, who in full devotion during some periods felt enclosed. Yet in the last few years something transcended and compensated for any limitations that devotion elicits. Eventually their working arrangement, their professionalism, their duties helped their personal friendship; their very intimacy began to assume an unusual tenderness.

In his last years Borges addressed love poems and dedicated publications to María. They traveled constantly. Once at daybreak they sailed together in a balloon over the Napa Valley. Of this voyage Borges spoke of his indescribable "felicity." He spoke to me now not of the error of that earlier marriage but of his love for María. Borges wrote, "María and I have shared the joy and surprise of finding sounds, languages, twilights, cities, gardens and people, all of them distinctly different and unique" (*Atlas*, 8). He read everything into the Moon, what the Persians called the mirror of eternity. In his new lyrics she was the Moon. When they were married at the end, it was only the world that might interpret this act as a Borgesian deed of paradox, as a gesture or something extraordinary. It bore no surprise. It was of course of legal importance, but in every other way by then nothing happened out of the ordinary. Their marriage, to use a phrase that Borges's Swinburne would have accepted, was already conceived and consummated in heaven.

When Borges entered the real labyrinth, the orginal stone one at Knossos, which has not departed from the Earth or time, he entered together with María and became lost. In a labyrinth one is lost; that is its purpose. But now he entered in the morning with María and was not lost alone. María took a photo of Borges sitting with his cane on the steps of the maze. Four fingers of his hand show a useless compass, pointing nowhere. But his blind eyes are wide open, looking toward María and her lens. Borges recorded being so lost with her and in time: "This is the labyrinth of Crete whose center was the Minotaur that Dante imagined as a bull with a man's head in whose stone net so many generations were as lost as María Kodama and I were lost that morning, and remain lost in time, that other labyrinth" (*Atlas*, 31).

Later, from my friend (Thomas) Anthony Kerrigan, the first (and the last) translator and editor of Borges's poems and fictions, I heard a few details about the months before his death. Tony was with Borges and María the last summer in Milan and the last December in Rome, just before they went to Switzerland.

In Milan Borges and María went to the season opening at La Scala, a serious social event. Hard-to-find tickets were given them by a wealthy princess whom Tony described as a Catholic Jew from northern Italy. When the couple entered the theater, Borges was recognized by the audience. There was spontaneous applause. Then the former president of the republic came and embraced Borges, followed by the incumbent president. It was a natural thing to do in Italy. As Tony related the event, my own eyes became misty. He sobered me up quickly by saying that Borges was bored stiff with *Aida*.

In later days in Rome, although Borges was sick, he gave no hint of the gravity of his disease. The teasing nobility, the outrageous behavior continued as ever, perhaps enhanced by his knowledge of the impending last act. His old claim of physical cowardice was exposed for what it was, a humorous mask behind which lay the stoicism he praised in the Socrates of the hemlock. To Tony he recited at odd moments, for no apparent reason, Dante Gabriel Rossetti's lines,

> Look in my face; my name is Might-have-been;
> I am also called No-more, Too-late, Farewell;

Only later did Kerrigan catch the obvious message of goodbye, which as a gentleman, as a man of letters, Borges would only let be overheard, though insistently:

> I am called No-More, Too-late, Farewell.

As in a story where the clue lay in the writing on the leopard's hide, he had to disguise his intent for the sake of later decipherment. He spoke his farewell through the mirror of Dante Gabriel Rossetti.

After Rome, in summer 1986 Borges and María went to Geneva. They would roam no more. Borges had lived there during his formative years toward the end of World War I. There he learned French and German; there he began to write in French and Spanish and published his first essay (in French). Geneva was always for him a city of return. Now Borges knew he had left Argentina for good.

The couple continued their literary collaboration in Geneva. As he recalled his youth there, the city where he had discovered Rimbaud and German and the verse of Heine, Borges was also unusually nostalgic about Buenos Aires. Even when in Argentina he was, like Antonio Machado, a poet of remembrance. So his work was at once a historical memory of a sea-roaming Anglo-Saxon sailor, of Poe contriving his atrocious marvels, Whitman prostrate on his white bed in his poor man's room, a public library, Victoria Ocampo, the writer friends, and then his own recollection of childhood Palermo, the Barrio Norte, and especially the *milonga* (a fast Argentine tango) and those *compraditos* who peopled the *milongas,* that is, the outsiders, the *orilleros,* the petty thieves, whorehouse guests, and the knife fighters.

Borges held to a strange notion deeply mingled with sexual machismo and orgasmic death: that dueling with pistols or swords is a foreign evasion from immediate courage, that boxing is a Greek sport, not a primitive agon, and that only Argentine knife fighting among fearless gang members outside a night bar reflected the truly desperate alienation he admired. Even after he had rejected the military for their shallow patriotism and national savagery, the knife fighter of his youth, of the 1890s just before his birth, became a criminal hero meriting fame and remembrance, whose blade should remain more glittering than respectable marble. He would resurrect that ghost. Even at the jammed talk-and-question session before a Harvard, MIT, and Boston University audience in spring 1980, the last question I took was a request for Borges to read a poem. He chose to recite a sonnet evoking the knife fighter Juan Muraña who was in his heroic prime in the 1890s. Borges said he felt he knew him personally. It was amazing to see the gentle wise man smilingly celebrate, with nostalgic passion, the life of the assassin Juan Muraña, "Whose craft was courage." Anthony Kerrigan's translation re-creates the Spanish:

Allusion to a Ghost of the Eighteen-Nineties

Nothing. Just Muraña's knife.
Only the truncated story on a gray afternoon.
I don't know why this assassin I never saw
Walks with me at twilight.
Palermo was lower down. The yellow
Prison wall loomed above
The suburbs and the quarter. Through that wild
Part walked Muraña, the sordid Knife.
The Knife. His face has been erased
And all I can recall of that austere mercenary,
Whose craft was courage,
Is a shadow and the flash of steel.
May time, which blurs out marble,
Keep sharp this name: Juan Murana.

In Geneva Borges had developed a lifelong intellectual friendship with Simon Jichlinski and Maurice Abramowicz. A few years earlier he had met Abramowicz again after fifty years and they continued their conversations about French symbolism, the Jewish origin of the Portuguese name Borges, and other matters, as if no time had elapsed since their last meeting. He was a Jew and Borges, as we know, had been accused of being a Jew during World War II, when Argentina was pro-Axis. At that time he claimed it was his lifelong quest to be of the culture of the Golem and of the Kabbalah, to be worthy of the *converso* Jewish blood in his veins. Earlier, Borges had written stories set in Geneva, often containing the double, a theme common to his work. Geneva was his double for Buenos Aires. A year before he died he wrote of death and his return to Geneva, "I know I will always return to Geneva, perhaps after the death of my body" (*Atlas*, 368).

In 1984, when he received word in Buenos Aires that Abramowicz had died in Geneva, he wrote an elegiac prose poem whose ending was a prescription of spirit for his own death: "This night you have told me without words, Abramowicz, that one should enter death as one walks into a fiesta" (*Los conjurados*, 36). The last dramas of his life were to be enacted in this Swiss city.

By this time it was known that Borges was planning to wed María. He was near death. Then untoward events took place. His sister, Norah, and her two sons objected to the marriage. Borges was always fond of Norah, whom he esteemed as an artist, and fond of his nephews. But now the family raised an ugly campaign against María, privately and in the Argentine newspapers.

Marcos Ricardo Barnatán, the Argentine poet and author of several volumes on Borges, told me in Madrid the following information. I repeat the facts, if they are so, without change or comment.

The final offense to Borges came when he discovered that his own bank account, to which his family had access, had, in anticipation of the marriage, been emptied of most of its contents. At this, Borges altered his will, leaving his entire estate to María. To the others he left "amplio lugar en la tumba en la Recoleta" (ample space in the tomb at La Recoleta Cemetery).

Borges and María were married in Geneva.

An Argentine friend of his and a professor from Oberlin College, Ana Cara-Walker, spent some days with the couple in early June. With the American poet and scholar David Young, Cara-Walker had been translating Borges's six *milongas*. These ballads were an accomplishment very dear to the poet, but their translations were devilishly elusive. Cara-Walker was consulting Borges about his lowlife heroic songs. Borges, she observed, was as usual dressed in a fine suit, yet, because of his frailty, he wore slippers rather than shoes. His humor and cunning erudition were as always. María had found an attractive apartment in the Vieille Ville, the section that Borges had always loved. Cara-Walker helped them move and Borges was delighted with his new home with María, its quiet seclusion and rooftop view of the pastel buildings.

Ana again saw Borges, but by now he could not leave his bed. That afternoon María was describing the walls of the bedroom with its beautiful wood paneling the color of sand, and Borges was taking in his newfound riches. Cara-Walker offers us a picture of María and the poet resting peacefullly, memorizing the room as his chosen companion gave him eyes: "She guided Borges's hand over the panel molding. . . . Satisfied with María's description, he lay back and fell into silence. 'Are you all right, Borges?' María asked. 'Yes,' he answered. This is the happiest day of my life.' " Cara-Walker left. By the time her plane reached New York on June 16, Borges was dead. She later wrote that Borges "entered death like a feast, with courage, lucidity, and happiness" (Cara-Walker, 8, 9).

Released from habit, from the weight of waking again to the obligation of being Borges, the poet was free. Wisdom, if not divinity, served him until the border of darkness. For many of us, the planet is indescribably lighter because of his physical departure. There is an emptiness of living anecdote, lightning wit, compassionate presence. Yet his favorite pastime, memory, also conspires in others to return not only the person but the letter. Does the letter give us his own conjectural truth? Does it tell us his "final South American destiny"? On some ruinous afternoon, is there in the missing letter and the mirror of the night "the unexpected mien of eternity"? In his "Conjectural Poem" as elsewhere, Borges will not tell us all, and even when he observes the thunder and the rainbow, his own example is enough. If at that border of silence Socrates knew something or nothing, Borges knew the same. But on the way, Borges mingled wisdom with laughter, added the genius and elegance of his unique word to the alchemy, and enhanced the mystery.

The deathbed marriage and Borges's own death soon thereafter left María doubly devastated: she experienced the loss of Borges even as she felt the calumny against her, which continued in the Argentine press for many months, only to be followed by unsuccessful lawsuits to break the will. She stayed on in Geneva, then went to Paris, to New York for business, but was initially unwilling to go back to Argentina. Eventually she did return to Buenos Aires, temporarily.

The romance of Borges and María was the last creation in Borges's life. The old *antiperonista*, the anti-fascist Argentine during the war, the Spinoza of Maipú Street had died without a Nobel Prize, yet some fundamental aspect of this most metaphysical author was satisfied. The isolation of his being, the ignorance inherent in public language and in any ultimate word, in the second that would usher in the routine nontime after death — all these unknowns, along with his days and nights, he was now sharing, in a formal pact of love, with his other voice, María.

In the last decade of his life, Borges became an itinerant sage. *Kim* had always been one of his favorite books, one of his "habits," as he would say. He knew Kipling's words by heart, as he did the Old English texts. Now he had a kinship with the itinerant Kipling hero. In all this wandering, in his *charlas,* Borges developed a special oral literature. Because of his blindness, his memory, his sagacity, his humor and nimble tongue, his love for repartee, his magical presence, Borges inevitably grew into a modern Socratic figure.

There is a well-known tradition of the sage whose work is spoken. The Buddha, Jesus, Lao-tzu, Socrates not only did not care to limit their thoughts by fixing them on a page, but also desired to avoid the danger of having their words turn into doctrine. Our record of these sages is largely from others who recorded with the instruments of the time: memory and the hands of scribes.

The Chinese Taoist Lao-tzu, who may actually have been three people or simply a tradition of quietism, is said to have ridden off one day on a water buffalo into the desert, where he dictated his poems and parables. Borges continued to dictate poems, parables, essays, and stories until the end, but increasingly his new medium was the *charla,* the modern dialectic. In those dialogues with his questioning colleagues and audiences, he created a public testament for our time. It did not differ in quality, intensity, and range from his personal dialogues with friends, which during most of his adult years had been his Chinese *tao,* his way of sharing the unwritten word. In the walks, the shared meals, and conversations, there is the voice of the blindman. Resonant, laughing, surprising. Opposing, intimate, profound. Equating the universe with a word, deciphering the alphabet of time. Despairing, spoofing. The voice that embraces the other.

The voice of the blindman is the essential Borges. Those who have heard him remain affected for life.

Works Cited

Barnstone, Willis, ed. *Borges at Eighty: Conversations.* Bloomington: Indiana University Press, 1982.

Borges, Jorge Luis. "An Autobiographical Essay." In *The Aleph and Other Stories, 1933–1969,* ed. Norman Thomas di Giovannni in collaboration with the author. New York: E. P. Dutton, 1970.

———. *Borges, a Reader: A Selection from the Writings.* Ed. Emir Rodríguez Monegal and Alastair Reid. New York: E. P. Dutton, 1981.

———. *Borges oral.* Buenos Aires: EMECE Editores/Editorial de Belgrano, 1979.

———. *La cifra.* Madrid: Alianza Tres, 1982.

———. *Los conjurados.* Madrid: Alianza Tres, 1985.

———. *Labyrinths: Selected Stories and Other Writings.* Ed. Donald A. Yates and James E. Irby. New York: New Directions, 1964.

———. *Obra poética, 1923–1977.* Ed. Carlos Frías. Buenos Aires: EMECE, 1972.

———. *Selected Poems, 1923–1967.* Ed. Norman Thomas di Giovanni. New York: Delacorte, 1968.

———. "The Wall and the Books," trans. Irving Feldman. In *A Personal Anthology,* ed. Anthony Kerrigan. New York: Grove Press, 1967.

———. in collaboration with María Kodama. *Atlas.* Trans. and annotated by Anthony Kerrigan. New York: E. P. Dutton, 1985.

———. edited with Silvina Ocampo and A. Bioy Casares. *The Book of Fantasy.* New York: Viking, 1988. (Translation of *Antología de la literatura fantástica.* Buenos Aires: Editorial Sudamericana, 1940)

———. "A Vindication of Basilides the False." In *Borges, a Reader: A Selection from the Writings.* Ed. Emir Rodríguez Monegal and Alastair Reid. New York: E. P. Dutton, 1981.

Burgin, Richard. *Conversations with Jorge Luis Borges.* New York: Holt, Rinehart and Winston, 1969.

Cara-Walker, Ana. "A Death in Geneva: Jorge Luis Borges, 1899-1986." *World Literature Today* (Winter, 1988): 5–11.

Guilbert, Rita. "Jorge Luis Borges." In *Seven Voices.* New York: Alfred A. Knopf, 1973.

Kerrigan, Anthony. "Autobiography." In *Contemporary Authors.* Vol. 11. Detroit: Gale Research Co., 1989.

Kodama, María. "Oriental Infuences in Borges's Poetry: The Nature of the Haiku and Western Literature." In *Borges the Poet*, ed. Carlos Cortines. Fayetteville: University of Arkansas Press, 1986.

Monegal, Emir Rodríguez. *Jorge Luis Borges: A Literary Biography*. New York: E. P. Dutton, 1978.

Physiologus Theobaldi Episcopi de Naturis Duodecim Animalium. Bishop Theobald's Bestiary of Twelve Animals. Latin text with translations. Lithographs by Rudy Pozzatti. Bloomington: Indiana University Press, 1964.

Visuddhimagga (Way of Purity). In Radhakrishnan, *Indian Philosophy*, I, 373. In Jorge Luis Borges, *Borges, a Reader: A Selection from the Writings*. Ed. Emir Rodríguez Monegal and Alastair Reid. New York: E. P. Dutton, 1981.

Index